Prevention and youth crime

Is early intervention working?

Edited by Maggie Blyth and Enver Solomon

**CENTRE FOR CRIME
AND JUSTICE STUDIES**

KH

First published in Great Britain in 2009 by The Policy Press

The Policy Press
University of Bristol
Fourth Floor, Beacon House
Queen's Road
Bristol BS8 1QU
UK
Tel no +44 (0)117 331 4054
Fax no +44 (0)117 331 4093
E-mail tpp-info@bristol.ac.uk
www.policypress.org.uk

North American office:
The Policy Press
c/o International Specialized Books Services
920 NE 58th Avenue, Suite 300
Portland, OR 97213-3786, USA
Tel +1 503 287 3093
Fax +1 503 280 8832
e-mail info@isbs.com

ISBN 978 1 84742 263 7

British Library Cataloguing in Publication Data
A catalogue record for this report is available from the British Library.

Library of Congress Cataloging-in-Publication Data
A catalog record for this report has been requested.

Cover image courtesy of www.johnbirdsall.co.uk
Cover design by Qube Design Associates, Bristol
Printed in Great Britain by Marston Book Services, Oxford

4/15/13

Contents

Foreword

The Association of Directors of Children's Services (ADCS) is the leadership organisation for children and young people's services. Members are charged with ensuring localities' cooperation to achieve the Every Child Matters outcomes. This 'duty to cooperate' covers statutory agencies: health, police, probation, services for young offenders, Learning and Skills Councils and local authorities. We expect that by 2009 it will include schools and colleges. ADCS works with government departments, from the Department for Children, Schools and Families and the Department for Innovation, Universities and Skills to the Home Office, the Ministry of Justice and Cabinet Office, to influence policy.

At the seminar from which this report has resulted, I made many of the points in its chapters: about the balance between early intervention, risk, and the potential for the public denigration of children and young people who offend through an enhanced focus on them as a group. I reflected on how far local authorities should bear the costs of incarceration. I was clear that we would welcome this shift of accountabilities if it came with both the resources currently expended and an expectation that we would use them differently.

Most directors of children's services (DCSs) are responsible for services for youth justice services, and at the same time for the universal and targeted services through which children and young people who offend may pass: schools, youth services and others. Holding all these strands together places DCSs in a unique position: we see what a young person lives with, and through, from every angle.

ADCS welcomed the government's Youth Crime Action Plan and its positive emphasis on early intervention and integrated approaches. We stressed the need to persevere with early intervention and to build on existing best practice. We urged a mandatory link between children's trusts and all youth justice services; a greater focus on positive publicity, for a nation frightened of its own next generation; and the greater involvement of the magistracy and judges in reshaping how we deal with, and how society views, those brought before them.

We are central to the work still to be done, and will continue to be held accountable for its results. This collection is both a timely and valuable contribution to the ongoing dialogue, in which we all need to remain engaged.

Maggie Atkinson, President, ADCS

Acknowledgements

We would like to thank everyone who contributed to this publication, including those who participated in a seminar in April 2008, which introduced many of the volume's themes. We are also grateful to the Barrow Cadbury Trust for providing financial support to the seminar and to the Centre for Crime and Justice Studies for its help in organising the event. Finally, without the support of the Youth Justice Board for England and Wales, we would not have had the opportunity to produce and distribute this volume, which we hope will enable practitioners and policy makers to reflect on the development of early intervention work.

List of abbreviations

ADHD	attention deficit hyperactivity disorder
ASB	anti-social behaviour
BME	black and minority ethnic
DCLG	Department for Communities and Local Government
DCSF	Department for Children, Schools and Families
FFT	functional family therapy
FIP	family intervention project
FNP	Family Nurse Partnership
HAC	Home Affairs Committee
IIP	intensive intervention project
ITYSS	integrated and targeted youth support services
MST	multi-systemic therapy
MTO	Moving to Opportunity [US government programme]
Nacro	National Association for the Care and Resettlement of Offenders
NEET	not in education, employment or training
OJJDP	Office of Juvenile Justice and Delinquency Prevention
PET	positron emission tomography
PSA	Public Service Agreement
PTSD	post-traumatic stress disorder
SSLP	Sure Start Local Programme
UN	United Nations
UNICEF	United Nations Children's Fund
YCAP	Youth Crime Action Plan
YIP	Youth Inclusion Programme
YISP	Youth Inclusion Support Panel
YJB	Youth Justice Board
YOI	youth offender institution
YOP	Youth Offender Panel
YOT	Youth Offending Team

Notes on contributors

Rob Allen is Director of the International Centre for Prison Studies at King's College London. He was previously Director of Rethinking Crime and Punishment at the Esmee Fairburn Foundation in London and, before that, Director of Research at the National Association for the Care and Resettlement of Offenders (Nacro) and Head of the Juvenile Offender Policy Unit in the UK Home Office. He was a member of the Youth Justice Board for England and Wales (YJB) for several years. He has extensive experience of international penal reform work, mainly in the field of young people.

Maggie Blyth is the Independent Chair of Nottingham Youth Offending Team (YOT) Management Board and has been a member of the Parole Board for England and Wales since 2005. She was Head of Practice at the YJB from 2001 to 2005 and set up the Oxfordshire YOT in the late 1990s. With a background in the probation service and youth justice, she continues to work extensively at international, national and local levels, advising on youth justice policy and practice. She is co-editor of *Young people and risk* (The Policy Press, 2007) and *Young people and custody* (The Policy Press, 2008).

Karen Clarke is Senior Lecturer in Social Policy in the School of Social Sciences at the University of Manchester. Her research is concerned with family policy in the UK, shifting state–family boundaries in relation to responsibility for children and young people and the implications of family policies for gender roles.

Felicity de Zulueta is a consultant psychiatrist and psychotherapist at the Maudsley Hospital, London, where she works as the lead clinician in the Traumatic Stress Service. She is also an adviser on personality disorders for the Department of Health. An Honorary Senior Lecturer in Traumatic Studies at the Institute of Psychiatry, she has published papers on the subject of post-traumatic stress disorder and violence from an attachment perspective. She is author of *From pain to violence: The traumatic roots of destructiveness* (Wiley, 2006).

Barry Goldson is Professor of Criminology and Social Policy at the University of Liverpool. He is the founding editor of *Youth justice: An International Journal* (Sage), and his most recent books include *In the care of the state? Child deaths in penal custody in England and Wales* (with D. Coles; Inquest, 2005), *Youth crime and justice: Critical issues* (with J. Muncie; Sage, 2006), *Comparative youth justice: Critical issues* (with J. Muncie; Sage, 2006) and the *Dictionary of youth justice* (Willan, 2008). He is currently compiling and co-editing, with Muncie, a three-volume set of international major works on youth crime and juvenile justice for the Sage Library of Criminology.

Judy Nixon is Principal Lecturer in Anti-Social Behaviour Studies at Sheffield Hallam University. She was a founder member of the established housing law research team and has extensive experience of researching and writing in the fields of urban policy and sociolegal issues, specialising in work around anti-social behaviour. Recent research projects include a major three-year evaluation of family intervention projects funded by the Department for Communities and Local Government, a study for the Home Office evaluating 'what works' for victims and witnesses of anti-social behaviour, and work for the Joseph Rowntree Foundation examining the use of reward schemes to stimulate greater tolerance of the visible presence of young people. She is currently working on an evaluation of the impact of Housing Benefit sanctions on families and, in collaboration with Professor Hal Pawson at Heriot-Watt University, a two-year evaluation of intensive family intervention schemes in Scotland designed to break the cycle of disadvantage.

Sadie Parr is a research fellow at the Centre for Regional, Economic and Social Research at Sheffield Hallam University. Her recent research has explored the role of family support in the governance of anti-social behaviour and she has written widely on the subject. More generally, she is interested in the convergence of social and criminal justice policies.

John Pitts is Vauxhall Professor of Socio-Legal Studies at the University of Bedfordshire. He has worked as a special needs teacher, a street- and club-based youth worker, a youth justice development officer, a group worker in a young offender institution (YOI) and a consultant to workers in youth justice, youth social work, the legal professionals and the police in the UK, mainland Europe, the Russian Federation and the People's Republic of China. His research includes studies of the differential treatment of black and white offenders in the youth justice system, the violent victimisation of school students, interracial youth violence, and the contribution of detached youth work to the life chances of socially excluded young people and violent youth gangs in London. He is editor of the journal *Safer Communities* and his recent publications include *The new politics of youth crime: Discipline or solidarity* (Macmillan, 2003), *The Russell House companion to youth justice* (with T. Bateman; Russell House, 2005), 'Othering the brothers: black youth, racial solidarity and youth crime' (with S. Palmer; *Youth and Policy*, 2006) and most recently *Reluctant gangsters: The changing face of youth crime* (Willan, 2008).

Enver Solomon is Deputy Director of the Centre for Crime and Justice Studies, an independent charity affiliated to the Law School at King's College London. He previously worked as Head of Policy and Research at the Revolving Doors Agency, where he carried out an evaluation of the agency's link worker schemes with young people, and at the Prison Reform Trust where he authored reports on young adults in custody, foreign national prisoners, prison privatisation and prisoner representative councils. He has published work on crime and the media, knife and gun crime and recently co-authored a major analysis of the government's youth justice reforms, *Ten years of youth justice under Labour: An independent audit* (Centre for Crime and Justice

Studies, 2008). Prior to working on criminal justice policy, he was a journalist for the BBC.

Howard Williamson is Professor of European Youth Policy in the Faculty of Humanities and Social Sciences at the University of Glamorgan, Wales, and visiting Professor at the University of Hertfordshire. He previous worked at the Universities of Oxford, Cardiff and Copenhagen, as well as being a practising youth worker for over 20 years. He has contributed to youth policy development in Wales, the UK and across the countries of the European Union and the Council of Europe. He was a member of the Youth Justice Board from 2001 until 2008 and is a trustee of the Duke of Edinburgh's Award. He has published extensively on a range of youth questions, especially concerning social exclusion, including *The Milltown Boys Revisited* (Berg, 2004), a follow-up study of a group of men he first met 25 years earlier when they were young offenders in the mid-1970s. He was appointed CBE in the New Year's Honours 2002 for services to young people.

Introduction

Enver Solomon and Maggie Blyth

Prevention rather than cure is the obvious, common-sense approach to dealing with any problem and it is unsurprising that criminal justice policy has been driven by such an ideal. Shortly after entering government in 1997, New Labour embarked on what was seen by many commentators as a more holistic preventative model than its predecessor Conservative government had utilised, with the establishment of Crime and Disorder Reduction Partnerships. The distinguished criminologist, David Garland, described it as a 'preventive turn', reflecting an 'epistemological break' with the past (Garland, 2000). Prevention strategies quickly became embedded in the work of Community Safety Plans within local authorities. Initially, much of the work focused on situational crime prevention. But more recently there has been a much greater focus on early intervention projects and initiatives to target particular individuals as early as possible. Inevitably, this has been directed at children and young people who are considered to be 'at risk' of becoming the prolific criminals of the future.

The initial early intervention programmes directed specifically at children and young people were developed by the Youth Justice Board (YJB). Indeed, the YJB's inaugural conference held in May 1999 was called 'Catch them early'. Risk-based early intervention strategies were developed to be used by Youth Offending Teams (YOTs) to identify children on the cusp of crime. At the same time, social policy programmes, in particular Sure Start, were rolled out to provide early intervention support for families with preschool children living in deprived neighbourhoods. For Tony Blair, early intervention was considered to be a vital part of New Labour's social and criminal justice agendas. He took a personal interest in pushing forward the early intervention agenda, particularly towards the end of his premiership. In 2006 he gave two major speeches in which he made a strident case for extending the early intervention approach. Blair claimed that 'you can detect and predict the children and families likely to go wrong', arguing that 'instead of waiting until the child goes off the rails, we should act early enough, with the right help, support and disciplined framework, to prevent it' (Blair, 2006).

This volume brings together contributions from experts to critically examine government policy in relation to early intervention programmes that aim to support families and to prevent children and young people from offending. It examines the fundamental premise behind the government's argument that it is right to intervene early, considering the consequences and outcomes that help address social exclusion. The contributions raise some important questions about prevention strategies. Are targeted services and programmes impacting directly on the trajectory of deprivation and crime or simply drawing more children and young people unnecessarily into the criminal justice system? Is early intervention symptomatic of a creeping criminalisation of social policy whereby a coercive approach is used to force so-called problem families and their children to engage with services? If it is, is that necessarily wrong if it works? And what are the lessons for how services should be configured and delivered to ensure safe, secure and just communities? How are local people themselves engaged in crucial decisions about how to tackle crime and social problems, and how do we motivate those most detached from the mainstream to take advantage of support provided?

The early intervention agenda

The early intervention agenda has continued to be the focus of much political attention in the last 18 months. Gordon Brown's government has signalled that it wants to push ahead with tackling problems early on in children's lives even further than when Tony Blair was Prime Minister. In an interview with *The Times* in June 2008, the Home Secretary, Jacqui Smith, called for an expansion of family intervention work to prevent children as young as five years old from 'problem families' drifting into anti-social behaviour and crime. She said: 'It is part of the role of government not to wait till crime has been committed but, for the good of the wider community and the families themselves, to step in earlier when it is obvious to all agencies that this is the type of situation that can end in tragedy' (*The Times*, 28 June 2008).

The early intervention agenda is now a priority across government, re-orientating the focus of recent years on 'respect' and anti-social behaviour. A Youth Taskforce, based in the Department for Children, Schools and Families (DCSF), took over from the Respect Taskforce in 2007 with a specific focus on prevention. The Youth taskforce action plan, published in March 2008, set out plans for early intervention and prevention 'alongside tough enforcement' (DCSF, 2008a). It made the case for dealing with 'emerging problems before they become serious and entrenched', unveiling 20 new intensive intervention projects (IIPs) providing 'non-negotiable intervention in order to prevent future anti-social behaviour' for 'a thousand of the most challenging young people' (DCSF, 2008b). The projects are based on the 65 family intervention projects (FIPs) that have been operational in England and Wales since 2007, targeting anti-social families with contractual support using methods of assertive social work. In addition, the government's recently appointed Adviser on Neighbourhood Crime and Justice, Louise Casey, has published 30 proposals to engage communities in tackling crime, which include more work with parents (Casey, 2008).

Most recently, the Youth crime action plan (YCAP), published in July 2008, further develops the government's early intervention policies. The YCAP outlines plans to 'set in motion a step-change in the delivery of early targeted support for young people and families, encouraging the delivery of services which focus on early intervention for families with the greatest risk of becoming the high rate offenders of the future' (HM

Government, 2008, p 8). An explicit target has been set to provide additional funding and expert support to at least 40 families in each local authority where children are known to have behavioural problems and be in need of assistance to prevent them entering the youth justice system (HM Government, 2008).

There are three clear assumptions that underpin the government's early intervention approach discussed at different points in this volume. First, there is a view that the earlier the intervention the better. The government believes that risk factors can be clearly identified, justifying intervention from a very early age, and that it can and does work. Second, targeted rather than universal provision is the preferred option. Finally, coercive engagement, based on tough sanctions for non-compliance, is assumed to be necessary in order to change the behaviour of problem youth and their families. The language now is of 'non-negotiable support and challenge' (HM Government, 2008). The contributions in this volume critically appraise these assumptions and examine whether those families most in need of support will be able to benefit from appropriate interventions or whether there is a danger of criminalising crucial welfare support and thus marginalising those most in need.

The earlier the better?

Early intervention has become a defining feature of Labour's approach to youth justice, including children's services, and is increasingly central to the direction of many local authorities across England and Wales. Indeed, Nottingham was named 'early intervention city' in 2008, and in its recently published Local Area Agreement (One Nottingham, 2008), the Local Strategic Partnership, known as One Nottingham, sets out its focus and planning on early intervention. The stance taken is that to avoid entrenched problems later in adolescence and adult life it is never too early to intervene. Many practitioners working in the field of youth justice argue that offending needs to be nipped in the bud at the earliest age and are supportive of a national Public Service Agreement target to measure the numbers of children and young people entering the youth justice system for the first time over the period 2008 to 2011. Both social exclusion and crime are beginning to be seen by government as intergenerational problems, resulting in a cycle of deprivation and leading to the children of parents in prison being more likely to be drawn into the youth justice arena.

However, while there may be broad agreement that access to mainstream services should be prioritised for children, young people and their families in deprived areas, there is, as yet, no clear blueprint for early intervention work. And will investment in early intervention *guarantee* a reduction in youth crime and social exclusion? Karen Clarke (Chapter Four) reviews the evaluations of the Sure Start programme. These show that the programme has had a positive impact, particularly in relation to children's health, children's social behaviour and parenting. But in terms of tackling overall deprivation and reaching those families most disadvantaged, Clarke argues that it has not had the impact that was hoped. The YJB's Youth Inclusion Programme (YIP) and the Youth Inclusion Support Panels (YISPs), both designed to intervene with children and young people from the age of eight to prevent them from becoming the criminals of the future, have had mixed results. A quarter of children who had not been arrested before joining a programme were arrested after completing it. But, of those who had been arrested before starting the YIP, three quarters of them were arrested for fewer offences following completion (Morgan Harris Burrows, 2003).

It could be that while there is no guarantee that risk-based pre-emptive intervention will divert children from problematic behaviours, it can have some impact on frequency and seriousness of offending or anti-social behaviour. And this is very important. There are understandable concerns from some practitioners and academics, however, that early intervention within a youth justice framework undermines justice by subjecting innocent children to unnecessary criminalisation, social control and regulation. Barry Goldson (Chapter Six) argues that diversion from the criminal justice system itself is more effective than early intervention, which he considers counterintuitive in addressing problems. He cites evidence that labelling through early intervention leads to a correctional spiral, accelerating criminalisation as distinct from crime prevention. Early diversion, not intervention, should be the priority.

Felicity de Zulueta (Chapter Five) reminds us that early intervention programmes are based on the premise that the foundations of disorderly conduct result from poor parental attachment from birth. She presents evidence that the lack of a positive attachment can result in deep trauma, which can manifest itself in extremely violent acts in later life. Early intervention is required but must be rooted in wider social care, not derived from the youth justice system. Universal pre- and post-natal parenting support through home visiting nurse schemes are proposed as the most effective crime prevention tool. This, of course, has been the rationale behind the government's 10 Family Nurse Partnership (FNP) pilots.

Targeted versus universal provision

During Blair's administrations, and reiterated by Brown, New Labour has recast the argument of tackling poverty and disadvantage by choosing to target prevention and early intervention approaches at so-called hard-to-reach problem families. Karen Clarke (Chapter Four) sets out how this approach has reshaped the Sure Start initiative in recent years. The focus now is on the most socially excluded families 'and the identification and separation from the rest of the population of this problem minority'. In her view, Clarke suggests that this reflects a 'moral underclass conceptualisation of social exclusion', distinct from an explanation that emphasises material poverty and inequality. She highlights the challenges facing the new children's centres managed through local authority children's services. If they are to address material deprivation, they will need to prioritise the necessary resources and expertise to work with those children, young people and families most marginalised from the mainstream.

Many YOTs are now merging with youth services to form integrated and targeted youth support services (ITYSS) within children trust structures. This offers the possibility of greater integration between early intervention, prevention and youth justice work, using a risk-based approach to assess the level of intervention required. However, as YOT budgets, including prevention funding, become pooled with wider children's services, the challenge will be to ensure that those young people who are most at risk are prioritised in gaining access to universal provision, most notably education and health services.

At present, central government policy indicates that the identification and targeting of the dysfunctional, problem family is at the heart of the youth crime early intervention and prevention agenda. As the recently published YCAP indicates, this agenda may sit better outside the criminal justice agenda, with oversight of YOTs moving to children's services rather than remaining within criminal justice spheres (HM Government, 2008). The new plan puts much greater emphasis on the importance of parenting and family support through targeted provision such as the FIP. Judy Nixon and Sadie Parr (Chapter Three) examine the evaluations of a number of FIPs designed to provide support to problematic families involved in disproportionate levels of anti-social behaviour, and suggest that there are a number of factors that contribute to the overall effectiveness of parenting programmes.

Interestingly, the Labour government has been largely out of step with its international counterparts in its approach to prevention work with young people and their families at risk. Many European countries have chosen to use social policy as a means of crime prevention rather than targeting children and families through the criminal justice system. Rob Allen (Chapter Seven) draws on an evidence base from the European Union with an analysis of different programmes that focus on the family, incorporate education work and have a community focus. He urges policy makers to draw on the lessons learned internationally to inform the early intervention debate.

It is of course possible to combine targeted prevention programmes that focus on communities rather than individual families and are supported by universally available youth provision and employment programmes. John Pitts (Chapter Two) provides a blueprint for 12 elements of neighbourhood-level interventions designed to prevent violent youth gang activity, arising from work undertaken in Lambeth. Rather than the family being the focus of attention, the wider community afflicted by broader socioeconomic and cultural trends becomes the locus for multiagency activity. Pitts therefore challenges government and Conservative policy, which fixates on the actions and risks posed by individuals and their families, arguing that their behaviour cannot 'be separated out from the circumstances in which they live'.

Universal and targeted services are not necessarily mutually exclusive. Indeed, it is this message that Howard Williamson (Chapter One) reinforces on the new ITYSSs. As YOTs and youth services merge to form these new structures within children's services, he argues that there is an opportunity to create an early intervention model that provides both support and surveillance of those children and young people engaged in anti-social behaviour or criminal activity. He states that so long as services target, and reach, those youngsters most at risk in deprived communities, enabling them to engage with mainstream services, it is not important whether interventions are provided within a youth justice arena or a predominantly youth work model. Multiagency working, information exchange and a quality workforce are the ingredients for successful early intervention work.

Coercive engagement: the criminalisation of social policy?

It seems that social and criminal justice policy are being more closely subsumed into one policy arena. Support is no longer unconditional in a world where enforcement and prevention go hand in hand. The FIPs discussed by Judy Nixon and Sadie Parr (Chapter Three) are a good example of this. Clear boundaries are set for the families involved, with sanctions imposed if they are crossed. As Howard Williamson (Chapter One) suggests, this might be a positive move if it prevents young people from being drawn into crime and actually diverts them in the manner in which Barry Goldson (Chapter Six) indicates is necessary. However, there is a danger that any carrot and stick approach to current early intervention strategies will tip some young people and their families further over the edge and away from participating in effective neighbourhood and local services. Any engagement with services that is contingent on good, responsible behaviour, with sanctions applied to enforce compliance, may not be sufficient in encouraging young people to lead law-abiding lives.

Using coercive rather than voluntary engagement to deliver social interventions intended to address the causes of crime may not in the long term actually contribute to a reduction in crime and anti-social behaviour. If the new IIPs for young people (a type of junior FIP) announced by the Youth Taskforce during 2008 are merely premised around the notion of non-negotiable support, resulting in the imposition of another Anti-Social Behaviour Order (ASBO) if the package is refused, there may only be an increase in the numbers of young people entering the youth justice system. Of course, much depends on the judgement and discretion of frontline staff and the extent to which they use their professional skills to engage a young person. This is likely to be one of the interesting workforce development features of the new ITYSSs comprising YOT and youth service practitioners. As Nixon and Parr (Chapter Three) note from their evaluation of the delivery of the FIPs, the approach practitioners choose to take is pivotal as 'they may provide a critical opportunity for resistance, subversion and the exercise of personal agency'.

A new dawn for youth crime prevention?

The rapidly changing early intervention youth justice policy terrain suggests that prevention is the focus of far greater political attention than previously. Arguably, the government's two new plans, the Youth Taskforce Action Plan and the YCAP, combined with the reorganisation of targeted youth services and youth offending services and the extension of children's centres, signifies a rebalancing, with prevention now seen by government as the primary response to problem youth rather than merely punishment. For many working in the field of youth justice, this approach is a welcome development. But as the contributions in this volume highlight, the issues stir considerable debate. The outlook for early intervention may be more promising, but the evidence will need to be gathered and the data examined to ensure that services are truly effective in engaging children, young people and their families and, most important, that they contribute to a reduction, not an increase, in the numbers of children and young people caught up in the youth justice system.

References

Blair, T. (2006) 'Our nation's future – social exclusion', Speech hosted by the Joseph Rowntree Foundation, New Earswick, York, 5 September.

Casey, L. (2008) *Engaging communities in fighting crime*, London: Cabinet Office.

DCSF (Department for Children, Schools and Families) (2008a) *Youth taskforce action plan: Give respect, get respect*, London: DCSF.

DCSF (2008b) 'Government intensifies drive to tackle anti-social behaviour in young people by stepping in early', Press release, 18 March, www.dfes.gov.uk/pns/DisplayPN.cgi?pn_id=2008_0054

Garland, D. (2000) 'Ideas, institutions and situational crime prevention', in A. von Hirsch, D. Garland and A. Wakefield (eds) *Ethical and social perspectives on situational crime prevention*, Oxford: Hart Publishing.

HM Government (2008) *Youth crime action plan 2008*, London: COI.

Morgan Harris Burrows (2003) *Evaluation of the Youth Inclusion Programme*, London: YJB.

One Nottingham (2008) *Local area agreement*, www.onenottingham.org.uk

Integrated or targeted youth support services: an essay on 'prevention'

Howard Williamson

Introduction

There is a lot of mischief within the debate on the respective merits and effectiveness of 'universal' versus 'targeted' services – of any kind. This is, of course, not a new debate; it has been around since the beginning of state-provided welfare services. Two burning issues have always informed that debate: one is concerned with the best use of scarce resources, the other with reaching the 'target' group. The two are intertwined: too much prescription and expectation about 'measuring' how effectively resources have been used is likely to produce what is sometimes described as 'perverse behaviour', in that providers will cherry-pick from within a broad target group (or even outside it) in order to optimise their chances of fulfilling the criteria on which they are being measured. This is what has been referred to, somewhat facetiously but with considerable accuracy, as 'hitting the target but missing the point'.

The point is that, in relation to any 'target' group but here in the context of young people, services should actually reach and have the desired impact on them. Over the past decade or so, this has produced a particularly polarised debate between, on the one hand, some sections of what might be called the traditional youth service, which has continued to advocate for universality, and, on the other hand, new policy approaches such as youth crime prevention. The latter makes its case on the basis of quasi-scientific assessments of 'risk' in order to identify those who should be the priority recipients of its interventions. In England, the now somewhat discredited Connexions Service sought to find a path between the two, using the rather cleverly constructed mantra about providing a 'universal service differentiated according to need', thereby being accessible to all but focusing its practice at the sharp end on young people most in need of its support – which, in its policy context, were those young people not in education, employment or training (NEETs).

Beyond the rhetoric of Connexions, the battle lines have been drawn, with strategies for attack and defence on both sides. The universalists argue their moral high ground of voluntary engagement, educative and developmental intent, and person-centred approaches. They attack the opposition for labelling and stigmatising young people and, of course, for missing some of those most in need because they do not fall into technically constructed frameworks of assessment. In reply, the targeters maintain that, although not an exact science, they can focus their efforts on young people who are both most in need and causing most public concern, help to keep them in good shape and divert them from the worst consequences of prospective risk behaviours. They attack the opposition for an absence of clear planning about their practice, failing to reach those most in need and operating largely with those who are already relatively included.

Policy makers have, arguably too often, sought to deflect or avoid this debate by redefining the territory and redesignating the names of the professionals: instead of 'youth worker', they become personal advisers, mentors, coaches or lead professionals. The service is no longer the 'youth service' but a kind of youth support service first flagged up in 1999 during the early Blair years. And yet the point I have made repeatedly is that good youth work has always exercised judgement in rationing time and resources in the direction of the more disadvantaged and more 'in need' young people, even if this has not been an explicit expectation. Similarly, even the most targeted practice within, for example, the youth justice system works best and is informed by some of the principles and processes that have historically been the bedrock of 'open' youth work. It is therefore perhaps useful to reflect for a moment on these two apparently different traditions of working with young people.

Youth work, youth justice – brief and biased histories

Youth work is routinely claimed explicitly to be about the personal development of young people and the 'social education' of the adolescent (Davies and Gibson, 1967). It may include, explicitly or implicitly, targeted work (see Spence et al, 2006). Its fundamental principles rest on concepts of universalism and voluntarism, or voluntaryism, as Davies (1999) put it. It is about a leisure or recreational space that young people choose to engage with, although it proclaims to have educative intent (see Smith, 1988). It thereby contributes to the learning and development, especially around 'soft skills', of young people.

Youth justice is explicitly about holding young people to account for their offending behaviour. It has undulated between more justice-focused responses, based on the paramountcy of offence criteria to justify interventions, and more welfare-focused responses concerned with the background and underlying social needs of the young offender (see Morris and McIsaac, 1978; Pitts, 2001; Smith, 2007). Interventions are specifically directed at the individual, whose compliance is compelled through the order of the court. It thereby contributes to both some form of proportional punishment and the rehabilitation of the individual.

Dispelling the mythology

Both of these brief accounts of youth work and youth justice are simultaneously mischievous and wrong, fuelling the fire of tensions between them. In fact, youth work has a long history of relating to major concerns of public policy, including youth crime. Indeed, a key moment in the development of the youth service related to wartime concerns about absent fathers and the prospect of burgeoning juvenile delinquency (see Jeffs, 1979; Davies, 1999). Before that, youth work had been concerned with child saving (social inclusion), character-building and contributing to the health of the nation. There had always been some element of *targeting*. Indeed, during the ministerial conferences on the youth service between 1989 and 1992, it was made quite clear that youth work could no longer invoke a 'scatter-gun' approach around vague claims about personal development and would instead be required to demonstrate its 'concentrated fusillade' on key youth questions, including youth offending.

Equally, youth justice had been concerned with the reconnection of young offenders to purposeful pathways to adulthood and adult citizenship: the borstal sentence established in 1908 was to equip young men with useful trade skills, and intermediate treatment in 1969 was about broadening the social opportunities and experiences of young people who breached the criminal law. More recently, summer SPLASH schemes and the Youth Inclusion Programme (YIP) have offered *universal* access, despite having some level of priority focus on specific individual young people.

So let us be extremely careful about any unequivocal location of youth work at one end of a spectrum and youth justice at the other.

A commitment to prevention and targeted youth support

Without any doubt, targeted prevention practice is rather more explicitly about meeting specific policy agendas, around issues such as youth crime, health-risk behaviours or drop-out from education and training. More person-centred developmental practice is not off-limits on these agendas, although it is sometimes less than explicit – possibly to satisfy the media's craving for tough-sounding rhetoric.

Although prevention and targeting can be traced sketchily back to the early days of social policy (not least with the crisp example, in the mid-19th century, of Mary Carpenter's work and the distinction between reformatories for incorrigible youth and industrial schools for those deemed capable of reform and rehabilitation), its recent emergence can be pinned to the mast of the work of Communities that Care (with its analysis of risk and protective factors) and the subsequent policy statements produced by the Social Exclusion Unit. The latter's work on young people, in particular in *Bridging the gap* (SEU, 1999) and then by the Neighbourhood Renewal Policy

Action Team 12 (SEU, 2000), was robust in its advocacy for a 'youth support service' and stronger prevention and early intervention. The Connexions Service was being developed at the time and has since been followed by a plethora of policy statements and initiatives throughout the UK and across a range of government portfolios – from children's services, through youth services to health and criminal justice. *Extending entitlement* (in Wales, see below) (NAW, 2000), *Transforming youth work* (DfEE, 2001), *Every child matters* (DfES, 2003), *Youth matters* (DfES, 2005), *Youth justice: The next steps* (Home Office, 2003), *Care matters* (DfES, 2007), the *Youth taskforce action plan* (DCSF, 2008), *The children's plan* (DCSF, 2007) and the *Youth crime action plan* (HM Government, 2008) are but some of these. They all speak persuasively to the same agenda, albeit from different starting points and with different vocabulary. Nevertheless, they proclaim that prevention is better than cure, that some groups identified as 'at risk' require and demand disproportionate levels of intervention, and that only an individualised or personalised response is likely to be effective. The most recent mantra is one of enforcement, resettlement and prevention, and, on the latter front, the joint sponsorship of the Youth Justice Board (YJB) by the children's and justice ministries from the summer of 2007 signifies an apparent commitment to the idea that the target group are 'children first, offenders second' (already enshrined in the All Wales youth offending strategy; WAG/YJB, 2004), demanding both youth service and youth justice.

Defining 'need' and the appropriate response

Political rhetoric is, of course, usually rather different from resource investment and practical action. There is invariably some contest between the principles and perspectives of professional practitioners and the expectations of politicians. And, rather than producing some convergence on issues around the 'troubled and troublesome', twin tracks can often appear (just as they did for Mary Carpenter two centuries ago). Thus, strategies for young offenders often swing between a focus on need, an assessment of risk, and attention to the frequency and seriousness of offending behaviour. In short, these could be reduced to different priorities for practice: help, control and punish. Once more, it would be easy to position youth work far away from such practice, yet there are certainly histories of youth work (especially in England, but also in other parts of Europe) that are bound up with the first two.

I would like us to think about both more generalist (youth work-based) youth practice and more focused (youth crime-based) youth practice as negotiating a path within different triangles of pressures and priorities. I have alluded to the 'need – risk – seriousness' elements of youth offending above: in most realities, they cannot be addressed separately except at a technical level. Lives are dynamic: as needs are addressed, presumably risk is lessened and the chances of serious additions to a criminal record are reduced. Professional practice is also dynamic and I have suggested elsewhere that, in youth work, there is a triangle involving professional principles, political priorities and the expressed needs/wants of young people to be negotiated. Getting stuck too close to any one corner of the triangle is likely to produce paralysis and incapacity (Williamson, 2006).

In both explicitly targeted work and more generalist practice (where more implicit 'targeting' still goes on), the question is not only about defining, identifying and assessing need but also about the knowledge, resources and capacity to meet it. The political framework for all contemporary policy initiatives (however targeted or not) tends to militate against the possibility of sustained effectiveness, as I suggest below.

Counting on success

There is a saying that not everything that can be counted is important, and not everything that is important can be counted. The preoccupation with outcomes and their measurement (verification) has been a challenge for both integrated and more targeted services. The contribution to the five Every Child Matters aspirations (in England), the seven 'core aims' (in Wales) and latterly the Public Service Agreement target for England about young people on the path to success has now to be demonstrated. Perhaps targeted practice stands a better chance of doing so simply because its constituency and 'clientele' are more uniform and homogeneous, and thus small steps are more readily identifiable. For youth work (non-formal education) it has proved more tricky, given a more heterogeneous population of young people, more eclectic practice, more unpredictable contact time and more diverse commitment by both young people and practitioners. Nevertheless, there have been recent claims that the initial *primary* (personal and psychological) change effected by youth work relationships and experiences provides the essential underpinnings for subsequent *positional* change – in terms of labour market engagement, family responsibilities, and desistance from substance misuse and crime (Banfield, 2008). It is quite possible that this is also what is going on in more targeted work; it is just that the counting rules are focused on more tangible and less visible effects. Whether these are the more important effects of either practice is another matter. We need to ask again and again what we are trying to measure, how we are planning to do this and, critically, when this is to be done. For both universal and more targeted youth services I favour at least some shift in attention to what is offered, to the quality of the interventions made: bad interventions are very likely to produce bad outcomes (and thereby make targeted programmes counterproductive in that they then strengthen social divisions and inequalities); good interventions will probably produce good outcomes, even if their character and timing cannot be predicted.

Learning the art of patience

The UK currently has a 10-year youth strategy – *Aiming high for young people* (HM Treasury, 2007). It was launched in July 2007 and is concerned with both integrated youth provision (somewhere to go, something to do, someone to talk to) and targeted youth support. The last government 10-year strategy for young people was the Children and Young People's Unit, launched in November 2000. It was abolished three years later!

The dispiriting aspect of this point is that both policy and practice *take time*. Policy takes time to 'bed in' and win the hearts and minds of those responsible for its delivery, whether old hands learning new tricks or new kids on the block. They themselves have to find effective methods of engaging with young people, building relationships and credibility, and establishing the direction of travel for which they are being paid. We may hear a lot of claims, almost certainly false, about faster ways of achieving these things but, whatever the description and depiction of 'work with young people', there are few shortcuts.

Such patience and incremental practice is not a luxury but a necessity for effective intervention, yet it has come to be treated by politicians as some kind of professional self-indulgence. The consequence has been described by Peter Hyman, once speechwriter for Tony Blair, as the 'tyranny of policy momentum' (Hyman, 2005) which, in turn, leads practitioners to develop coping strategies ranging from leaving the field, cherry-picking the quick wins, to doctoring their returns. Those who remain honestly in the field, if they are expected to reach the hard to reach, will reach only the least hard of the hardest to reach. Young people right on the edge will remain untouched and therefore unaffected. The point applies equally to generic youth work, expected to produce a certain number of accredited outcomes, and to targeted youth support, expected to return a certain proportion of the disengaged to education, training or employment.

Thinking sensibly

Conceptually, the starting point both for youth work in the 21st century and for targeted youth support may be in the wrong place. Where once youth work may have dealt with the 'acute anxieties of adolescence', now it is working in the context of the 'chronic crisis of young adulthood' (Williamson, 1985). Where once 'benign neglect' was the desired position for youth justice – avoid labelling, leave the kids alone and they will grow out of it – now this is tantamount to malign indifference, in the context of difficult transitions to adulthood and the ways in which social exclusion has a clustering and persisting effect. Where once family support and decent schooling were usually sufficient to confer advantage and positive futures on young people, today the picture is far more diverse and complex.

And this is the point. We should not be looking at troubled and troublesome teenagers but at 'sorted-out' young adults. We should ask ourselves what kind of 'package' of opportunities and experiences they have had in their lives to get them where they are now: active in the labour market and civil society, responsible within their families. The package does not require the thinking of Einstein, and there is usually remarkable consistency when people are asked what it should consist of: family support, good education, access to new technologies, attachment to youth organisations, opportunities in sport or music away from home experiences, international travel and exchange. There are other things. Some young people gain access to opportunities organically through their private networks or through their initiative in relation to public possibilities, but others will get very little if it is left to these processes. Public policy has to reach out to those young people in particular if the youth divide (Jones, 2002) is not to widen. If we fail in this task, we should not be surprised if our challenging 14-year-old remains excluded from school, delinquent, racist, homophobic and preoccupied with the immediate locality. And the task is for both general youth work (to promote broader access and experience) and targeted youth support (to make sure the most disadvantaged get the essentials). A primary target group is shared and the two approaches are complementary, not in opposition. (Incidentally, this is the thinking behind the 'flagship' youth policy in Wales, Extending entitlement [NAW, 2000], although it has been misinterpreted, distorted and corrupted since its launch in 2000 [see Williamson, 2007a].) The best approach to the prevention of 'pathology' is the promotion of competence and confidence, hope and belief, opportunity and possibility.

Ultimately it is about practice, not strategy

The tyranny of policy momentum has, regrettably, produced what the late Peter Clarke, the first Children's Commissioner in the UK (for Wales), called 'all flagships and no fleet' in a reference to the work of the Welsh Assembly Government. There can be a plethora of well-intentioned and well-constructed policies and strategies but without effective delivery mechanisms and suitably trained practitioners little is likely to be achieved. This is why, in 2006 in Wales, a fascinating piece of joint work between the Children's Commissioner and the Chief Constable of South Wales was produced. It mapped a blueprint for delivery at the local level and, significantly for this chapter, drew few distinctions between youth justice and youth service workers (see Towler et al, 2006). And this is the nub of the issue. I have argued for many years (see Williamson, 2007b, p 14), and it is enshrined in Policy Action Team 12 (SEU, 2000), that there is an inalienable case for 'critical people at critical moments'. Young people often *do* put their faith in adults. Practitioners need to be there when young people need them. Those trusted are often rather unlikely candidates, such as the teacher adulated by the young woman who hated teachers (Butler and Williamson, 1994). That teacher was accessible and responsive, unlike the social worker described by another young person in the same study who was never there when she was needed: she was always 'on leave, on the sick or on a training course'!

The message here, therefore, is that, ultimately, strategy and structures can only go so far. What is needed is what I have called 'advanced skill youth practitioners', following David Blunkett's embracing of what he announced as advanced skill teachers. In the end, their location within youth justice services or 'bog standard' youth work does not matter, so long as they understand that their professional responsibility is to find a meeting of the ways between supporting young people and the (educational re-engagement and youth crime prevention) aspirations and targets of public policy. Our most challenging young people both deserve and need sophisticated and experienced practitioners. Those who are more inexperienced will struggle to deal with the complexities of those young people's lives and may well end up subjected to ridicule and exploitation. The more sophisticated practitioner will have acquired the repertoire of options to know when – to invoke a driving analogy – to push on the brake and when to press on the accelerator. And in order to juggle those options effectively they also have to be vested with sufficient levels of discretion. This applies to both youth work and youth justice: the foundations may be laid in professional training but the infrastructure of effective practice can only come about through learning from diverse experience. Learner drivers are fine in good conditions but are likely to crash in adverse circumstances. Competent youth practitioners, within and beyond youth work and youth justice, will discharge their responsibility to three Rs: reach, relationships and relevance. And although politicians may not like to hear it, without appropriate investment both in professional training and in the exercise of judgement and discretion, these three Rs remain untouched and are replaced by cycles of deception and delusion (Williamson and Middlemiss, 1999). Neither youth justice nor youth work is exempted from this assertion.

Conclusion

In the brave new world of 'single plans for children and young people' (Wales) and integrated youth support services (IYSSs) (England), we are at risk of forgetting that it is usually immaterial who responds to young people's needs – so long as somebody does. Nor is the funding stream especially relevant; young people do not typically ask who is paying for their support or experience!

The policy high ground is currently occupied by those advocating targeted youth support based on a formalised assessment framework to determine the focus of intervention and governed by a robust approach to performance management. My experience, through practice, is that young people remain pretty adept at circumventing unwanted intervention and fairly responsive to engagement that seems to them to be credible and relevant. Thus, those old, currently rather discredited claims concerning relationships and trust actually remain extremely important as foundation stones for more tactical support and intervention. There is not the gulf assumed between quality youth work and more targeted practice. The absence of 'evidence' around the former is not necessarily evidence of absence. Very intangible – and very hard to measure – but important things may still be happening. There may be order within the perceived chaos of youth work. Indeed, youth work may acknowledge that its practice starts with something of a lack of focus and steadily works towards a sense of purpose. Precisely because more targeted work is proclaimed to have more scientific foundations, it works hard at concealing the confusion and uncertainties that are *always* an integral feature of practice with young people, especially more challenging and difficult young people.

Just as there was once an ideological conviction that universal services prevailed in effectiveness over more selective provision (George and Wilding, 1976), so it is equally misguided to advocate uncritically for targeted provision. There will *always* be questions about criteria, reach, engagement and impact. What is ultimately important is finding the balance between considering young people 'holistically', in the round (the conventional 'youth work' model), and being able to respond to specific needs and challenges (the 'targeted prevention' model). The latter, after all, is critical both for young people and for public confidence in the interventions directed at troubled and troublesome young people. Of greatest importance is not the means but whether or not desirable practice, opportunity and experience (as well as supervision and regulation, in some instances) ever reaches the young people at whom it is meant to be directed. Youth work has had a bad press in recent years and has been decimated by a succession of political decisions. Yet, if one probes carefully, one finds much of its character rather secretly still alive and kicking in a range of targeted initiatives. The problem is that if the mythology around effective practice continues to be sustained on more visible and superficial claims regarding targeted support, then it becomes less and less likely that sufficient reach will be exercised: with hard-to-reach young people (whether offenders, substance misusers or those excluded from school), practitioner discretion will remain critical to ensuring engagement and the best chance of 'success'. Premature expectations regarding that success and over-management of practitioner performance will guarantee, as Colley (2003) once put it, that defeat is snatched from the jaws of victory.

References

Banfield, L. (2008) *The contribution of non-formal learning to young people's life chances*, Leicester: National Youth Agency/Fabian Society.

Butler, I. and Williamson, H. (1994) *Children speak: Children, trauma and social work*, London: Longman.

Colley, H. (2003) *Mentoring for social inclusion: A critical approach to nurturing mentor relationships*, London: Routledge Falmer.

Davies, B. (1999) *A history of the youth service in England – Volume 1, 1939-1979: From voluntaryism to welfare state*, Leicester: National Youth Agency.

Davies, B. and Gibson, A. (1967) *The social education of the adolescent*, London: University of London Press.

DCSF (Department for Children, Schools and Families) (2007) *The children's plan*, London: DCSF.

DCSF (2008) *Youth taskforce action plan: Give respect, get respect*, London: DCSF.

DfEE (Department for Education and Employment) (2001) *Transforming youth work*, London: DfEE.

DfES (Department for Education and Skills) (2003) *Every child matters*, London: DfES.

DfES (2005) *Youth matters*, London: DfES.

DfES (2007) *Care matters: Time for change*, London: DfES.

George, V. and Wilding, P. (1976) *Ideology and social welfare*, London: Routledge & Kegan Paul.

HM Government (2008) *Youth crime action plan 2008*, London: COI.

HM Treasury (2007) *Aiming high for young people: A ten year strategy for positive activities*, London: The Stationery Office.

Home Office (2003) *Youth justice: The next steps*, London: Home Office.

Hyman, P. (2005) *One out of ten: From Downing Street vision to classroom reality*, London: Vintage.

Jeffs, A. (1979) *Young people and the youth service*, London: Routledge & Kegan Paul.

Jones, G. (2002) *The youth divide: Diverging paths to adulthood*, York: Joseph Rowntree Foundation.

Morris, A. and McIsaac, M. (1978) *Juvenile justice?*, London: Heinemann.

NAW (National Assembly for Wales) (2000) *Extending entitlement: Supporting young people in Wales*, Cardiff: NAW.

Pitts, J. (2001) *The new politics of youth crime: Discipline or solidarity?*, London: Palgrave.

SEU (Social Exclusion Unit) (1999) *Bridging the gap: New opportunities for 16-18 year olds not in education, employment or training*, London: SEU.

SEU (2000) *National strategy for neighbourhood renewal: Report of Policy Action Team 12: Young people*, London: SEU.

Smith, M. (1988) *Developing youth work: Informal education, mutual aid and popular practice*, Milton Keynes: Open University Press.

Smith, R. (2007) *Youth justice: Ideas, policy, practice* (2nd edition), Cullompton: Willan.

Spence, J., Devanney, C. and Noonan, K. (2006) *Youth work: Voices of practice*, Leicester: National Youth Agency.

Towler, K., Williamson, H., Battle, M. and Francis, D. (2006) *SOTODO – Someone to listen, something to do: An holistic multi-agency youth at risk prevention model for South Wales*, Swansea: Office of the Children's Commissioner for Wales/South Wales Police.

WAG/YJB (Welsh Assembly Government/Youth Justice Board) (2004) *All Wales youth offending strategy*, Cardiff: WAG.

Williamson, H. (1985) 'Struggling beyond youth', *Youth in Society*, no 98, January.

Williamson, H. (2006) *Youth work and the changing policy environment for young people*, Leicester: National Youth Agency.

Williamson, H. (2007a) 'Youth policy in Wales since devolution: from vision to vacuum?', *Contemporary Wales*, vol 19, pp 198-216.

Williamson, H. (2007b) *The thoughts of Chairman How!*, Leicester: National Youth Agency.

Williamson, H. and Middlemiss, R. (1999) 'The emperor has no clothes: cycles of delusion in community interventions with "disaffected" young men', *Youth and Policy*, no 63, spring, pp 13-25.

2

Intervening in gang-affected neighbourhoods

John Pitts

Introduction

Violent youth gangs are almost invariably located in economically distressed urban neighbourhoods. Innumerable US studies and recent experience in Europe and the UK mainland indicate that poor housing, material poverty and the absence of primary sector employment contribute significantly to the presence of violent youth gangs (Hagedorn, 1998; Sassen, 2007; Pitts, 2008). This suggests that neighbourhood-level interventions that endeavour to address both the problems afflicting these neighbourhoods and their broader socioeconomic and cultural determinants might serve to stem the flow of young people becoming involved in gang violence as victims and as perpetrators.

Why here? Why now?

From 1979, the post-war tendency towards a narrowing of the gap between rich and poor was reversed, resulting in the growth of both absolute and relative poverty. This income polarisation was mirrored in the housing market. The Right to Buy and Tenant Incentive schemes precipitated a 'secession of the successful' as the economically active vacated 'social housing' to be replaced by the socially disadvantaged (Hope and Foster, 1992). Whereas at the beginning of the 1980s the average household income of council house residents was 73% of the national average, at the beginning of the 1990s this had fallen to 48%. By 1995, over 50% of these households had no breadwinner (Power and Tunstall, 1995). By 1997, 25% of the children and young people under 16 years old in the UK were living in these neighbourhoods. In its report, *Bringing Britain together* (SEU, 1998), the Social Exclusion Unit identified 1,370 housing estates in Britain, which it characterised as 'poor neighbourhoods which have poverty, unemployment, and poor health in common, and crime usually comes high on any list of residents' concerns' (SEU, 1998, p 4).

Poverty

In 2008, in Lambeth, a London borough with one of the highest levels of gang-related violence in the UK, over 40% of children live on or near the poverty line. In 2001, in the Lambeth wards where gang activity was most prevalent, between 47% and 60% of children lived in families eligible for means-tested benefits (Income Support, Job Seeker's Allowance, Family Credit and Disability Working Allowance) (Pitts, 2008). The poorest ward in the borough is the stamping ground of the notorious PDC (Peel Dem Crew/Poverty Driven Children). In a national survey undertaken in 2000, this ward was ranked 431st of the 8,414 wards in England for child poverty, with an index score of 60.0, as against 88.7 for the Wirral (the highest) and 0.5 for Gerrards Cross North (the lowest). Eligibility for free school meals is often used as a proxy indicator of poverty. In 2002, 38% of the borough's children were eligible for free school meals, against a national average of 17%. In this ward, eligibility for free school meals was 52%.

Between 1984 and 1997, the numbers of young people aged 16 to 24 in the labour market shrank by almost 40% (Coleman, 1999). While, today, some of this number are to be found in government-funded, supply-side training programmes (notably the New Deal) and in higher education, the bulk are unemployed. These changes have had a particularly detrimental effect on black and minority ethnic (BME) young people aged 16 to 24, and young men in particular, who are substantially more likely than their white counterparts to be unemployed (36% of black Caribbeans, 31% of Pakistanis and Bangladeshis, 26% of Indians and 14% of white people) (ONS, 1998). Saskia Sassen (2007, p 103) observes:

> It is the downgrading of manufacturing that has played a crucial role in cutting off the bridges that used to enable low-income youth to move into reasonably paying jobs in a world of expanding, mostly unionised, factories. Now many of these jobs are gone or have been downgraded to sweatshop work, often drawing on immigrant workers. This cuts off one of the key ways for youth to mainstream themselves out of gang life. The result has been that gang members stay longer in gangs and are more likely to participate in the criminal economy.

While gang involvement is not the exclusive preserve of BME young people, they are, nonetheless, overrepresented. Although the 1980s and 1990s was a period of considerable upward educational and social mobility within Britain's BME communities, this was paralleled by a worsening of the predicament of large numbers of BME people at the other end of the social and economic scale (Robins, 1992; Power and Tunstall, 1995; Palmer and Pitts, 2006).

The early 1980s saw the flowering of a vibrant black voluntary sector, which spawned youth and community projects, supplementary schools, information and advice services, housing associations, the black press and a growing number of black-owned businesses (Palmer and Pitts, 2006). These projects facilitated economic investment in the black community and helped to open up legitimate economic opportunity for many black people living on or near the poverty line (Power and Tunstall, 1995). However, because many of these initiatives were dependent on government funding, from the mid-1980s, government cutbacks served to undermine the black voluntary sector, thus compounding the predicament of the poorer members of the black community (Owusu, 2000).

By 1995, 40% of African Caribbeans and 59% of Pakistanis and Bangladeshis in the UK were located in the poorest fifth of the population. This contrasts with only 18% of the white population (Power and Tunstall, 1995). In London, by the mid-1990s, up to 70% of the residents on the poorest housing estates were from ethnic minorities (Power and Tunstall, 1995) and levels of adult and youth unemployment were among the highest in the UK.

The neighbourhood effect

In certain multiply disadvantaged urban neighbourhoods, children, young people and their families are at heightened risk of gang involvement and gang victimisation. Indeed, US research suggests that neighbourhood of residence may be the key factor in determining whether or not a young person becomes involved in youth crime and youth gangs.

The Pittsburgh Youth Study (Wikstrom and Loeber, 1997), an analysis of the lives of over 15,000 young people in the city, found that offending by subjects with no, or very low, individual and familial risk factors occurred significantly more frequently in the lowest socioeconomic status neighbourhoods, and that the relation between these risk factors and serious offending 'breaks down' for those living in the most disadvantaged communities. These findings challenge what Elliott Currie (1985) calls the 'fallacy of autonomy', the idea that the behaviour of individuals and their families can be separated out from the circumstances in which they live.

Research into the fortunes of people who move from poor to more prosperous neighbourhoods indicates that they are more likely to become 'economically self-sufficient' and to earn higher salaries (Galster and Zobel, 1998; Leventhal and Brooks-Gunn, 2001). The results are similarly positive for their children. Findings from the US federal government's Moving to Opportunity (MTO) experimental mobility programme, for example, suggest that moving to socially mixed, 'non-poor' areas produces 'significant and positive effects on child and parent health, as well as on child behaviour and youth delinquency and on safety and exposure to violence' (Del Conte and Kling, 2001, p 3).

Some commentators argue that these remarkable changes are a result of 'movers' gaining access to labour markets (see, for example, McGahey, 1986) and that the spatial concentration of social disadvantage is a result of poor neighbourhoods becoming spatially segregated from local economies. Research also suggests that this economic segregation sets in train processes that further isolate these neighbourhoods because, as McGahey (1986) suggests, residents in poor, high-crime neighbourhoods tend to derive their livelihoods from the 'informal economy' and 'secondary sector' labour markets, characterised by low wages and sporadic, dead-end work supplemented by 'government transfers, employment and training programmes, crime and illegal hustles which constitute important additional sources of income, social organisation and identity for the urban poor' (McGahey, 1986, p 102).

As in the poorest neighbourhoods in Lambeth, another key characteristic of high-crime neighbourhoods is transience. Skilled, economically mobile adult workers leave, and their departure serves to further destabilise the neighbourhood, thereby deepening family poverty. McGahey (1986, p 102) writes:

> The quality and quantity of jobs in a neighbourhood determine the ways people form households, regulate their own, and the public behaviour of others, and use public services. The resulting neighbourhood atmosphere then helps to shape the incentives for residents to engage in legitimate employment or income-oriented crime. A high level of adult involvement in primary sector employment spawns stable households, stable families, stable social relationships and enhanced vocational opportunities for the next generation.

And, of course, a low level of adult involvement in primary sector employment produces the opposite.

A further characteristic of these neighbourhoods is that residents tend not to be connected to locally influential social and political networks. This denies them information about social, educational or vocational opportunities, as well as access to the political influence that could improve their situation (Morris, 1995).

It is not that people in these neighbourhoods have no 'social capital' but rather that their social capital tends to be 'sustaining but constraining', enabling people to 'get by', to survive the day-to-day struggle, but not to 'get on', by moving out of their present situation and into the social and economic mainstream (De Souza Briggs, 1998; Pettit and McLanahan, 2001).

Moreover, living in a poor neighbourhood, among what Detleif Baum (1996) has described as a 'discredited population', makes one the object of stigma and discrimination, undermining self-esteem and making one even less willing to move beyond the confines of the neighbourhood. Baum (1996, p 23) writes:

> Young people sense this discreditation in their own environment, in school or in the cultural or leisure establishments. Through this they experience stigmatisation of their difference, of their actions, and the perceived incompetence of the people

they live among. The options for action are limited and possibilities for gaining status-enhancing resources are made more difficult. At some stage the process becomes a self-fulfilling prophecy; young people and adults come to think that there must be 'something in it' when their characteristics and ways of behaving are stigmatised, and some become confirmed in this uncertainty.

Surveys have repeatedly shown that people who live in poor areas tend to condemn petty crime and benefit fraud (Dean and Taylor-Gooby, 1992). However, the struggles of everyday life in a poor neighbourhood can mean that they find it difficult to live up to their own values. They may therefore 'go along with', and in some cases benefit from, the criminality in the neighbourhood. This, in turn, contributes to the stigma that attaches to them and this, in turn, compounds their isolation. Moreover, it also gives an ambiguous message to young people who are involved in, or may be on the threshold of, criminal involvement (Kennedy, 2007).

Alternative cognitive landscapes

As we have noted, in the 1980s and 1990s, the situation of the poorest segment of Britain's BME community worsened significantly (Palmer and Pitts, 2006). The effects of structural youth and adult unemployment and family poverty were exacerbated by negative experiences in school and confrontations with the police on the street. As a result, many people in the black community made a link between their present situation and the racial oppression experienced by their forebears (Pryce, 1979). Their sense of being 'stuck' was compounded by the departure of the upwardly mobile, politically articulate sections of the black community (Pryce, 1979). To be socially excluded with the prospect of eventual inclusion may generate hope but, as the 1990s progressed, the situation of these black citizens, marooned on the social margins, appeared to be growing steadily worse (Power and Tunstall, 1995). Ben Bowling and Coretta Philips (2006) argue that such undeserved injustice generates frustration and rage, while David Kennedy (2007) says that it also promotes 'norms and narratives supportive of gang violence'. James Short (1997) argues that, over time, these norms and narratives foster 'alternative cognitive landscapes' in the minds of gang members. He writes:

Mutual suspicion and concern with respect pervade the ghetto poor community. Under such circumstances social order becomes precarious....

This seemingly inordinate concern with respect – resulting in a low threshold for being 'dissed' (disrespected), Anderson writes, 'can be traced to the profound alienation from mainstream American society felt by many inner-city blacks, particularly the poorest' (Elijah Anderson, 1990, p 1).

Out of concern for being disrespected, respect is easily violated. Because status problems are mixed with extreme resource limitations, people – especially young people – exaggerate the importance of symbols, often with life-threatening consequences.... These consequences are exacerbated by the widespread belief that authorities view black life as cheap, hardly worth their attention. This view is reinforced when black-on-white crime receives more attention by authorities and by the media than does black-on-black crime. The result is that people feel thrown back on their own limited resources. They arm, take offence, and resist in ways that contribute to the cycle of violence. (Short, 1997, p 203)

In these circumstances, as James Short (1997) has argued, wider cultural values become unviable and these young people come to occupy a far bleaker 'alternative cognitive landscape', developing what is sometimes called a 'soldier mentality', characterised by a heightened sensitivity to threat and a constant preparedness for action (Sampson and Lauritson, 1994). And this, as Decker and Van Winkle (1996) have demonstrated, tends to isolate gang members from the social and cultural mainstream to the extent that they can only feel at ease in the neighbourhood gang.

Malcolm Gladwell (2000) states the matter succinctly when he says that, given the choice, it is far better to come from a troubled family in a good neighbourhood than a good family in a troubled neighbourhood. Given what we know about the concentration of poverty, social and economic exclusion, infant mortality, teenage pregnancy, youth crime, violent youth gangs, drug dealing and educational failure in particular Lambeth neighbourhoods, the neighbourhood would seem to suggest itself as a focus for intervention.

Stemming the flow: the neighbourhood as a site of intervention

To a considerable extent, the problem of violent youth crime in these neighbourhoods is rooted in family poverty and the economic, educational, vocational, social and cultural marginalisation that characterises the lives of many gang-involved and gang-affected young people and their families. It follows that, while in the short term an effective strategy will endeavour simply to reduce the risk of death and injury, in the medium to long term it will develop a multi-agency infrastructure capable of combating the economic, educational, vocational, social, cultural, neighbourhood and familial factors that place local children and young people at risk of gang involvement and violent victimisation. Such a strategy has at least 12 elements.

Family support

Culturally relevant family support is a central prop of initiatives to reduce violent youth crime. Many parents whose children are gang-involved or gang-affected feel unable to exert the care, control and influence they would wish and this often engenders a sense of inadequacy, which can, in turn, undermine their coping capacities. This can lead to family conflict, and in some cases young people may vacate, or be 'thrown out' of, their homes. These parents need support. Yet statutory support for the parents is usually only forthcoming if they are made the subjects of a, potentially stigmatising, 'parenting order' imposed by a court.

The House of Commons Home Affairs Committee (2007) report on black young people and the criminal justice system recommends that statutory agencies make greater use of third sector organisations that offer parenting programmes, in particular, black voluntary, community and faith organisations. However, for this to become a reality, it will be necessary to build the capacity of these groups and organisations. Where they are effective, these organisations tend to have built from the 'bottom up', offering non-stigmatising, culturally relevant support to parents under pressure.
Support from the clergy may also be regarded by recipients as less stigmatising and more acceptable because of their religious and spiritual, as distinct from statutory, affiliations. From autumn 2007 the National Parenting Academy has offered practitioners advice and training on work with families of African and Caribbean origin. Families may need support with the nuts and bolts of daily life and, in particular, help in finding out about the state benefits to which they are entitled, their rights regarding state services and, in some cases, advocacy in the areas of benefits, housing, education and childcare. Beyond this, they may also need help with financial management and information about the educational, recreational and vocational opportunities available to them. Moreover, parents under these sorts of pressures often experience a sense of isolation, even though other parents in their neighbourhoods are subject to the same pressures. This is one of the reasons why neighbourhood capacity building has often grown out of work with parents and has become a central feature of some effective gang interventions.

Neighbourhood capacity building

It is clear that in some neighbourhoods there are pressures on children and young people to become gang-involved. It would follow that one element of any intervention aiming to stem the flow of young people into violent youth gangs should aim to help residents combat these pressures. Neighbourhood capacity building utilises existing social networks to connect with neighbourhood residents with in-depth knowledge of their area, its inhabitants and the problems they confront. It endeavours to enable people to exert greater control over the policies affecting their neighbourhood and the practices of the professionals within it by equipping them with the relevant knowledge and skills, while opening up access to the places where key decisions affecting them and their neighbourhood are made.

Residents on gang-affected estates are often fearful for their children and themselves because of the threat posed by neighbourhood gangs; this is why few residents are currently willing to come forward as witnesses when violent crimes are committed. Following a serious assault on an estate in East London, parents, with the support of the housing association, started a project called 'Reclaiming our estate, reclaiming our children'. This involved discussion with the police, the local authority and children and young people on the estate, some of whom were gang-involved, about residents' attitudes to violent behaviour and how a safer neighbourhood might be achieved. In some areas, Police Safer Neighbourhood Teams have been the lead agencies in encouraging local people to express their concerns. However, for local people to give unequivocal messages to gang-involved young people and information about gang activity to the police and other agencies, both key elements of the successful Operation Ceasefire I in Boston, Massachusetts (Pitts, 2008), they must have confidence that those agencies are prepared to remain involved until the threat has abated, and also that police powers will be used fairly. In Boston the police expended a great deal of effort in trying to regain the trust of residents in gang-affected neighbourhoods, at one point becoming prime movers in improving social, sporting and recreational provision.

Many residents also feel blamed for the problems of which they are in fact the victims, feeling that their voices are unheard in the places where key decisions about their plight are made. This would suggest that the high-profile involvement of local politicians acting as advocates for people in gang-affected neighbourhoods could be central to the success of any such initiative.

As we have noted, the predicament of residents is compounded by stigma and isolation. An important part of capacity building in these neighbourhoods will therefore concern reconnecting residents with educational, training, recreational and vocational opportunities beyond the neighbourhood.

Educational interventions

Many schools in gang-affected neighbourhoods are dealing with the adverse effects of gang culture on their students, as well as struggling with problems of truancy, student–student and staff–student conflict and school exclusion. There is, moreover, a disproportionately large number of black and mixed heritage children and young people experiencing problems of truancy, exclusion and underachievement. These issues are highlighted in the 2007 House of Commons Home Affairs Committee (HAC) report on young black people and the criminal justice system. It points to the importance of disciplinary measures in schools being seen to be fair and the committee heard that some, otherwise able and compliant, students were absenting themselves from school because they believed they had been unfairly treated by a member of staff. The report suggests that this issue should be a focus of school inspections and that the government should implement the findings of the Department for Education and Schools priority review, which gave additional guidance and training for school leaders and staff on reducing exclusions and meeting their responsibilities under the 2000 Race Relations (Amendment) Act to eliminate unlawful discrimination and promote equality of opportunity and good relations.

The HAC report notes that proper provision should be made for children and young people excluded from school and that alternatives to exclusion should be explored. To this end, it suggests that government should research the impact of supplementary schools, provided within the black community, and promote cooperation and collaboration between supplementary schools and mainstream schools.

Faced with a similar problem among Maghrebian young people in Anderlecht (Brussels, Belgium), the municipality introduced a mediation scheme into secondary schools and vocational colleges (Pitts and Porteous, 2005). The rationale for this was that second- and third-generation Maghrebian children and young people were not only excluded from the sociocultural, educational and economic mainstream, they were also estranged from their parents and their culture of origin. Thus, there was a need for people who understood these difficulties and 'had a foot in both camps' to help bridge the gap.

Mediators drawn largely from the Moroccan community were appointed. These mediators had a loose accountability to the head teacher or college principal, but were employed by the municipality to vouchsafe their independence. They owed their primary allegiance to the child or young person, and their job was to be liaison agents and communication facilitators between teachers, students and school management. The mediators also had an important role to fulfil as intermediaries between the school and any part of the outside world, such as the police or potential employers, with which students were likely to come into contact. As time went by, the list of their duties grew to include individual monitoring of students in difficulty and establishing partnerships and projects in the neighbourhood. The responsibilities cited most often by mediators were:

- mediating between young people involved in violence;
- mediating between young people and the school in the case of truancy;
- facilitating communication between teachers and students;
- facilitating communication between schools and families;
- working with the psychological/medical/social services, students and families;
- keeping contact with students in conflict with the school;
- handling the individual monitoring of students; and
- keeping contact with students who had dropped out.

The Anderlecht initiative has made a significant impact on violent youth crime in the neighbourhood, drop-out rates, educational attainment and employment. Professionals and politicians involved in the initiative attribute its success to the following factors:

- It is holistic. It addresses social, cultural and economic factors simultaneously.
- It involves students as partners in developing the initiative.

- It engages professionals in a process of change, adaptation and dialogue with students.
- It reconfigures professional boundaries in order to ensure that appropriate mixes of skills, knowledge and authority are brought to bear on problems.
- It uses mediators to develop partnerships between the key stakeholders and to articulate a range of individuals, services and resources into the 'minimum sufficient network' (Skynner, 1971) necessary to address the complex problems confronted by the children and young people.

Like the HAC report, the REACH report, produced in August 2007 by The Men's Room, commends reducing the barriers faced by black parents and families by building stronger parent–teacher relationships and that this should be achieved via 'a national framework of family–school partnerships, ensuring that the specific needs of Black families are integral to the framework' (DCLG, 2007, p 49). It also argues for increasing parental engagement, creating of parent-centred learning workshops and encouraging more black parents to become school governors, teaching assistants and teachers.

Like the REACH report, the HAC report recommends mentoring support in schools and indicates that it should be targeted at primary/secondary transfer. However, mentoring is something of a catch-all term and in any such initiative it would be important to distinguish between 'correctional mentoring', which aims, primarily, to make good deficits within the mentee, and emancipatory mentoring, wherein the mentor, having made the journey themselves, helps the mentee navigate their path through a hazardous social and economic environment.

As we have noted, schools are adversely affected by gangs, and many are struggling to counter the influence of gang culture and the effects of living in gang-affected neighbourhoods on their students. It would therefore be important for gang-affected schools to be involved in any violent youth crime initiative.

Employment and enterprise

The high level of black and mixed heritage youth unemployment in many inner-urban neighbourhoods, its contribution to young people's decision to affiliate to gangs and their failure to desist from membership point to the centrality of robust, coherent and creative employment strategies to effective gang interventions.

Current employment policy is founded in the notion that work is the best way out of poverty and labour market intervention is increasingly targeted at the more disadvantaged groups. A new national skills strategy is emerging, designed to tackle extensive shortfalls in the levels of skills needed by the UK workforce. Neighbourhood renewal is being refocused, with a greater emphasis on tackling worklessness. Social housing policy is acknowledging that for communities to be stable over the longer term requires social landlords and their tenants to tackle very high levels of worklessness and benefit dependency. The London Learning and Skills Council, for example, recognises the need to address non-participation and lower than average levels of attainment for young people.

Recent community consultation has confirmed widespread support for measures of this type. There seems to be no lack of commitment, effort or resources to tackle low levels of participation and attainment and high levels of worklessness. However, there is frequently a mismatch between skill levels and the available opportunities. The obvious response is to 'upskill' these young people. However, those most in need of these types of interventions are, in many cases, already disaffected and unlikely to take advantage of them.

This suggests a need for targeted interventions that offer alternative routes into attainment and work at an earlier stage. These interventions need to be:

- attractive, offering real opportunities for work in the local labour market;
- built, as far as possible, on the successful elements of existing good practice and resources available in the borough;
- as dissimilar as possible from traditional learning and training;
- based in individual aspiration and assessment of need; and
- backed up by mentoring or one-to-one support over a significant period of time – for as long as it takes.

The government is planning to raise the age at which people are required to engage in education or training to 18. Meanwhile, funding for training is passing into the hands of local authorities. However, disaffected, gang-involved young people will need a labour-intensive, creative and sometimes unorthodox approach if they are to remain in education or training. Interventions designed to offer an alternative, work-oriented route for disaffected young people should build on the best practice developed within community, public authority and private sector agencies and organisations. Such initiatives would, ideally, be guided by a small group of credible local organisations that would ensure that high-quality opportunities were available and all known means were being utilised to reach this 'hard-to-reach' target group.

Youth and community provision

One of the most successful and best-evaluated gang intervention programmes in the US is the Comprehensive Gang Strategy devised in 1993 by the US Department of Justice's Office of Juvenile Justice and Delinquency Prevention (OJJDP). This involves long-term programmes that target both gang-involved young people and those who are, or may become, at risk of gang involvement. The programmes target young people who are unable to connect with legitimate social institutions and aim to provide individualised, age-appropriate social opportunities to them on the basis of an assessment of their needs and abilities.

At present, youth and community work responses to gang-involved and gang-affected young people are somewhat disparate. Some target young people heavily involved with gangs and gun crime, while others respond to the fears, needs and ambitions of children and young people growing up in gang-affected neighbourhoods. However, it is evident that, despite the important work they are doing, these programmes seldom represent a comprehensive gang initiative. There are a number of reasons for this:

- the paucity and uncertainty of the financial support available to them;
- a shortage of skilled and trained personnel;
- a lack of coordination of their efforts;
- competition between agencies;
- the absence of information-sharing protocols with the police and other criminal justice agencies;
- a lack of relevant, up-to-date intelligence about gang activity that would enable them to mount sustained, targeted interventions in particular neighbourhoods/ locations;
- the absence of a shared risk/needs assessment framework with which to devise interventions for targeted groups and individuals; and
- the absence of a systematic programme of monitoring and evaluation to serve as a basis for decisions about service provision.

What is needed, however, is a comprehensive 'layered' youth work intervention that is both preventative and responsive, targeting both those involved in gang and gun crime and those affected by it (see Table 2.1).

At Level 1, interventions would target core gang members known to the police and their unapprehended associates, via Persistent and Prolific Offender (PPO) and Intensive Supervision and Surveillance (ISSP) programmes and by third sector gang 'Exit' programmes operating outside, and independent of, the criminal justice system. It is at levels 1 and 2 that discussion with the police concerning the relative merits of enforcement action or social intervention in any given case would take place.

At Level 2, a useful vehicle for interventions with youngers and certain wannabees at serious risk of heavy involvement in gangs would be the type of Youth Inclusion Programme (YIP) introduced into 70 high crime neighbourhoods in 1999 by the Youth Justice Board (YJB) for England and Wales. The YIP targets a core group of 50 young people, deemed by a multi-agency panel to be those most 'at risk'. In addition to the core 50, a broader group of up to 150 young people, usually friends or associates of the core group, is encouraged to participate in YIP activities. As with Level 1 interventions, interventions at Level 2 would focus on intensive problem solving, mediation and the development of alternative futures via education, training and employment. However, YIPs utilise a broad range of methods, including street-

Table 2.1: A four-level gang intervention model

	The intervention	The target group
Level 1	The police/Persistent and Prolific Offender (PPO)/Intensive Supervision and Surveillance (ISSP) and specialist third sector Exit programmes	Targeted intensive interventions with core gang members (elders/youngers)/prolific violent offenders. Interventions would include enforcement and/or intensive social intervention involving problem solving, mediation and the development of alternative futures via education, training and employment
Level 2	Dedicated neighbourhood-based Youth Inclusion Programmes (YIPs)/extended school/further education colleges/university Aim Higher programmes and specialist voluntary/third sector organisations	Targeted interventions with younger gang members and those on the periphery (wannabees) but seriously 'at risk' of involvement. Interventions would involve intensive problem solving and the development of alternative futures via education, training and employment
Level 3	Statutory youth service outreach team/Youth Inclusion Support Panel (YISP)	Targeted interventions with moderately 'at-risk', gang-involved groups, (tinys) and younger siblings. Problem-oriented and social-educational interventions
Level 4	Housing associations/schools/sports clubs/voluntary/third sector organisations, eg ORIGIN, Flipside, Lambeth Young People's Service	Area/school-based social-educational/recreational youth and community interventions directed towards gang-affected young people

Source: Pitts (2008)

based youth work, counselling, mentoring, group work, outdoor activities, football tournaments, fashion shows and so on and in doing so manage to make and sustain contact with what is often a multiply disadvantaged and 'hard-to-reach' population. As well as enhancing their social lives, YIPs aim to reintroduce these young people to education, training or work (Morgan Harris Burroughs, 2003). However, effective employment opportunities have to play to the cultural strengths of the young people they are aimed at and may involve basic skills education on the one hand and training people to become self-employed business people on the other.

At *Level 3*, interventions would target those on the periphery of gang involvement, who would be unlikely to find their own way into education, training or employment.

This level of intervention would aim for reintegration into, or support for participation in, mainstream educational, recreational and vocational activity, probably utilising mediators.

At *Level 4*, interventions would consist of 'universal' social-educational and recreational youth and community work, but with a particular focus on non-gang-involved children and young people, under pressure in gang-affected neighbourhoods.

Rehabilitation and resettlement

Adequate throughcare and aftercare arrangements for gang-involved young people when they return from penal institutions are a key feature of effective gang initiatives. Successful rehabilitation depends on the quality of the work undertaken during the prison sentence and in the period following release, as well as on close liaison between the prison and the youth offending or probation services. Research indicates that desistance from future offending is most likely if, on release, the young person's family situation is stable, they have somewhere decent to live, they have fulfilling work yielding an adequate income, that any substance abuse problems are addressed and that they have access to social networks that offer non-criminal social and recreational opportunities (Farrall, 2002). There are particular pressures on returning gang members from their own and other gangs and, of course, there is the ever-present temptation of easy money from the drugs business. It is for this reason that these young people may need a great deal of support during re-entry and this support may also involve finding them accommodation outside their neighbourhood to avoid these pressures (Bateman and Pitts, 2005). Effective intervention with returning gang members therefore requires coordination of a number of different agencies and the nomination of a key worker who will work with them intensively. This level of intervention may be beyond the capacities of the youth offending or probation services and it may therefore fall to project workers from gang-desistance programmes to provide it. The intensity of such work would therefore need to be recognised in project funding and the training and support offered to project workers.

Shared ownership and leadership

The OJJDP Comprehensive Gang Strategy is based on the assumption that gangs become a chronic problem in communities where key organisations are inadequately integrated and sufficient resources are not available to target gang-involved youth. It also assumes that community mobilisation will be a prerequisite of success and that local citizens and organisations will be

> involved in a common enterprise ... working as a team. This is important because to remain anchored in day-to-day reality, and achieve the necessary credibility, the

initiative must have representation from, and ready access to, local young people and adults caught up in the gang problem. It is important therefore that such involvement goes beyond tokenism since the evidence suggests that genuine political participation can serve to reduce crime and violence in the poorest neighbourhoods. (Crimmens, 2004, p 18)

Sherry Arnstein (1969) (see Figure 2.1) provides a salutary 'ladder of citizen participation' against which to measure the degree of participation to be ceded to the subjects of an intervention.

If the partnership is to flourish, it will be important that the initiative is not perceived as being located administratively within the criminal justice system or in an organisation concerned primarily with crime reduction/prevention, since this may well deter participation by would-be community activists and young people who are, or who have been, involved in gang activity.

Moreover, perceived criminal justice connections might well provoke a negative response from those young people targeted by the initiative. Indeed, the HAC report observes that the success of Exit programmes appears to be related to their clients' perceptions of whether or not they are separate from criminal justice agencies.

Figure 2.1: A ladder of citizen participation

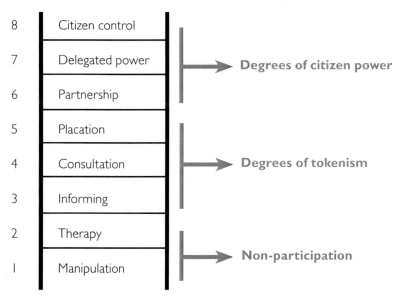

8	Citizen control	
7	Delegated power	Degrees of citizen power
6	Partnership	
5	Placation	
4	Consultation	Degrees of tokenism
3	Informing	
2	Therapy	
1	Manipulation	Non-participation

Intelligence, assessment and targeting

The development of a comprehensive violent youth gang strategy will require accurate, up-to-date information about the activities of individuals and groups within gang-affected neighbourhoods. It would therefore be necessary to collect and collate data on gang-involved young people, young people at risk from gangs and gang-affected neighbourhoods. Initially, it would be necessary to undertake research to establish the names, membership and location of gangs and offending youth groups, in order to assess threats, risks and needs, as a prelude to identifying targets for intervention, which would, in turn, determine the types of programmes to be commissioned.

Alongside this, there would be a need to create, adopt or adapt a shared risk/needs assessment framework with which to devise interventions for targeted groups and individuals.

Monitoring and evaluation

In order to steer and develop an initiative with gang-involved and gang-affected young people, independent monitoring and evaluation of interventions and their impact is crucial. However, it is now fairly widely accepted that the modes of research and evaluation utilised extensively in the justice system in recent years, which measure only inputs and outcomes and reveal little about how and why change occurs, are of little use to service users, policy makers, managers or practitioners. Moreover, there is growing evidence that applied research is most effective where service users, managers and practitioners feel they have some ownership of the research process. By involving these activists it becomes possible to discover not just whether a particular intervention 'works' or not, but how and why it works and whether, and if so how, the lessons learned might be generalised to other settings. A further advantage of this approach is that it can give service users an opportunity to formulate the questions to be asked and develop skills in research fieldwork and data analysis.

Commissioning and funding

There is a need to ensure the adequacy and duration of funding necessary for effective and sustained intervention and the transparency and rationality of commissioning and funding decisions. For this to happen, funding and commissioning decisions would need to be made in the light of the intelligence data on service need and evaluation data on project or programme effectiveness.

Project infrastructure

Although it is generally agreed that community and faith groups would be central to effective gang strategies, most lack the kinds of infrastructure that enable effective project management. This can serve as a disincentive to these groups to embark on new ventures. In the recent past, funding regimes have worked against the development of 'grassroots' community organisations and they have had a particularly deleterious effect on the black voluntary sector. Short-term funding, a sometimes complex bidding process, lack of money to pay for independent monitoring and evaluation and the requirement to produce lengthy final reports, along with day-to-day administrative tasks such as employment, salaries, National Insurance, tax and so on have discouraged the participation of these groups.

In order to address this problem, there is a need for a central facility that would employ specialist workers to undertake programme support services (writing bids, commissioning, monitoring and evaluating, writing final reports) in partnership with small voluntary, community and faith groups. This facility would also employ and train young people and adults from gang-affected neighbourhoods, linking them into relevant courses in further and higher education. It would, in addition, provide 'back office' clerical services (salaries, National Insurance, tax, accounts and so on).

Youth and community work training

Effective gang work requires a critical mass of young 'road people', but for them to be effective it is necessary to create adequately resourced and academically accredited structures to handle their recruitment, training and professional supervision. In order to address this problem, there is a need for a central facility, available to all projects involved in the initiative, to play a training and staff supervision/staff development role with young 'road people' and other volunteers or trainees appointed by the commissioned agencies. This training function would be developed in partnership with training providers in further and higher education to ensure that volunteers and trainees receive forms of accreditation that enable them to progress to education and training in relevant fields.

Conclusion

This chapter offers a sketch of some of the components of a medium- to long-term, comprehensive intervention in gang-affected neighbourhoods. But however good these components might be, such interventions will come to nothing unless the partners stick together, and stick with the task, until 'the job is done'. Indeed, it may be that some of the components outlined here will need to become a permanent fixture in these neighbourhoods. A decade of more or less ineffective 'quick fix', 'what works' initiatives in youth justice also tells us that if the related problems of social exclusion, crime, disorder and violence are to be tackled, resources must be diverted out of what is sometimes optimistically described as 'effective offender management' into serious and sustained prevention in the places where they are fermented.

References

Anderson, E. (1990) *Street wise: Race, class and change in an urban community*, Chicago, IL: University of Chicago Press.

Arnstein, S. (1969) 'A ladder of citizen participation', *Journal of the American Planning Association*, vol 35, no 4, pp 216-24.

Bateman, T. and Pitts, J. (2005) *The Russell House companion to youth justice*, Lyme Regis: Russell House Publishing.

Baum, D. (1996) 'Can integration succeed? Research into urban childhood and youth in a deprived area of Koblenz', *Social Work in Europe*, vol 3, no 3.

Bowling, B. and Phillips, C. (2006) *Young black people and the criminal justice system: Submission to the Home Affairs Committee Inquiry*, October.

Coleman, J.S. (1999) 'Social capital in the creation of human capital', in P. Dasgupta and I. Serageldin (eds) *Social capital: A multifaceted perspective*, Washington, DC: World Bank Publications.

Crimmens, D. (2004) *Having their say*, Lyme Regis: Russell House Publishing.

Currie, E. (1985) *Confronting crime: An American challenge*, New York: Pantheon.

DCLG (Department for Communities and Local Government) (2007) *REACH: An independent report to government on raising the aspirations and attainment of Black boys and young Black men*, London: DCLG.

Dean, H. and Taylor-Gooby, P. (1992) *Dependency culture: The explosion of a myth*, Hemel Hempstead: Harvester Wheatsheaf.

Decker, S.H. and Van Winkle, B. (1996) *Life in the gang: Family, friends and violence*, Cambridge: Cambridge University Press.

Del Conte, A. and Kling, J. (2001) 'A synthesis of MTO research on self sufficiency, safety and health and behaviour and delinquency', *Poverty Research News*, vol 5, no 1, pp 3-6.

De Souza Briggs, X. (1998) 'Brown faces in white suburbs: housing mobility and the many faces of social capital', *Housing Policy Debate*, vol 9, no 1, pp 177-221.

Farrall, S. (2002) *Rethinking what works with offenders, probation, social context and desistance from crime*, Cullompton: Willan.

Galster, G. and Zobel, A. (1998) 'Will dispersed housing programmes reduce social problems in the US?', *Housing Studies*, vol 13, no 5, pp 605-22.

Gladwell, M. (2000) *The tipping point*, New York: Little, Brown & Co.

Hagedorn, J. (1998) *People and folks: Gangs, crime and the underclass in a rustbelt city*, Chicago, IL: Lakeview Press.

Hope, T. and Foster, J. (1992) 'Conflicting forces: changing the dynamics of crime and community on a problem estate', *British Journal of Criminology*, vol 32, no 4, pp 488-504.

House of Commons Home Affairs Committee (2007) *Black young people and the criminal justice system*, Second report (HC 181-I), London: HAC.

Kennedy, D. (2007) 'How to stop young men shooting each other', Presentation to the Metropolitan Police Authority, New Scotland Yard, March.

Leventhal, T. and Brooks-Gunn, J. (2001) *Moving to opportunity: What about the kids?*, Mimeo, New York: Columbia University.

McGahey, R.M. (1986) 'Economic conditions, neighbourhood organisation and urban crime', in A.J. Reiss and M. Tonry (eds) *Communities and crime*, Chicago, IL: Chicago University Press.

Morgan Harris Burrows (2003) *Evaluation of the Youth Inclusion Programme*, London: Youth Justice Board.

Morris, L. (1995) *Social divisions: Economic decline and social structural change*, London: UCL Press.

ONS (Office for National Statistics) (1998) *Report on GSS survey activity in 1998*, GSS Methodology Series (www.statisticsauthority.gov.uk/).

Owusu, K. (2000) *Black British culture and society*, London: Routledge.

Palmer, S. and Pitts, J. (2006) 'Othering the brothers: black youth, racial solidarity and gun crime', *Youth and Policy*, no 91, pp 5-21.

Pettit, B. and McLanahan, S. (2001) 'Social dimensions of moving to opportunity, *Poverty Research News*, vol 5, no 1, pp 7-10.

Pitts, J. (2008) *Reluctant gangsters: The changing shape of youth crime*, Cullompton: Willan.

Pitts, J. and Porteous, D. (2005) 'Nobody should be alone', *European Journal of Social Work*, vol 8, no 4, pp 435-50.

Power, A. and Tunstall, T. (1995) *Swimming against the tide: Polarisation or progress*, York: Joseph Rowntree Foundation.

Pryce, K. (1979) *Endless pressure: A study of West-Indian lifestyles in Britain*, Bristol: Bristol Classical Press.

Robins, D. (1992) *Tarnished vision: Crime and conflict in the inner cities*, Oxford: Oxford University Press.

Sampson, R. and Lauritson, L. (1994) 'Violent victimisation and offending: individual, situational and community-level risk factors', in A. Reiss and J. Roth (eds) *Social influences: Understanding and preventing violence*, vol 3, Washington, DC: National Academy Press.

Sassen, S. (2007) 'The global city: one setting for new types of gang work and political culture', in J. Hagedorn (ed) *Gangs in the global city*, Chicago, IL: University of Illinois Press.

SEU (Social Exclusion Unit) (1998) *Bringing Britain together: A national strategy for neighbourhood renewal*, The report of Policy Action Team 12: Young people, London: SEU.

Short, J. (1997) *Poverty, ethnicity and violent crime*, Boulder, CO: Westview.

Skynner, R. (1971) 'The minimum sufficient network', *Social Work Today*, August.

Wilkstrom, T. and Loeber, R. (1997) 'Individual risk factors, neighbourhood SES and juvenile offending', in M. Tonry (ed) *The handbook of crime and punishment*, New York, NY: Oxford University Press.

3

Family intervention projects and the efficacy of parenting interventions

Judy Nixon and Sadie Parr

Introduction

Over recent years it has been apparent that New Labour's anti-social behaviour agenda has changed in focus and emphasis, with increasing attention being paid to control measures involving 'whole family' approaches and parenting interventions. Family intervention projects (FIPs), first pioneered by the Dundee Families Project in the mid-1990s and subsequently developed by a small number of English local authorities in 2003-04, now have a central role in the government agenda to foster a 'new approach to the most challenging families' (Home Office, 2006a; Cabinet Office, 2008). In 2006, the establishment of a network of 50 FIPs formed a core part of the *Respect action plan* (Home Office, 2006a), while, more recently, cross-government commitment to this model of working is evidenced in a number of policy initiatives including the Social Exclusion Task Force review of 'families at risk' and the recently published *Youth taskforce action plan* from the Department for Children, Schools and Families (DCSF, 2008) with the roll-out of intensive intervention projects targeting young people.

As the number and type of FIPs have grown,[1] a recurring theme evident in FIP working practices is the need to reduce the impacts of parental problems on children's life chances, with measures to improve parenting skills frequently forming a core element of FIP practices (Dillane et al, 2001; Jones et al, 2005; Nixon et al, 2006a, 2006b). This focus on 'parenting deficit' is symbolic of a significant expansion of state intervention into family life and signals a renewed emphasis on the domestic sphere as the site for policy interventions (Lister, 2006). Whether family-based interventions are to be welcomed as a means of facilitating new possibilities for genuinely positive practice or whether they are more correctly located as a component of an increasingly interventionist and punitive youth justice model is open to question (Goldson and Jamieson, 2002; Holt, 2008; Parr, 2008; Parr and Nixon, 2008).

This chapter seeks to contribute to the debate about the benefits and drawbacks of increased state intervention in family life through an examination of the lived material realities of FIP practices viewed through the lens of parents' (usually mothers'[2]) experiences. It will draw on rich qualitative data collected as part of three evaluative research studies of FIPs involving eight separate projects (Nixon et al, 2006a, 2006b; Parr, 2007; Nixon and Parr, 2008; Parr et al, 2008). In particular, data will be drawn from over 87 semi-structured interviews with family members working with the projects and subject to parenting intervention. All the qualitative interview data were transcribed and subject to detailed analysis using a standard coding frame, with special attention paid to identifying negative cases and counter-tendencies.

The chapter is divided into three sections. The first section starts with a brief description of FIPs and discusses how they might be located as a form of 'early intervention'. It outlines which families form the target group for this type of intervention before providing a detailed examination of project practices as they relate to parenting skills training. Reflecting on parents' views on the impact of parenting interventions, in the second section of the chapter we seek to explore what it is about engaging parents in parenting/household skills training that might work to improve young people's life chances, focusing on the family and local contexts within which project practices have been developed. The chapter concludes with a discussion that raises questions about the sorts of models of parenting that are being promoted, the purpose of parenting skills training and who really benefits.

What are family intervention projects?

Prevention, early intervention or 'last chance saloon'?

Each of the projects included in the research formed part of locally developed anti-social behaviour (ASB) strategies that recognised the interrelated nature of prevention, enforcement and supportive action. They were designed principally to provide families at risk of eviction due to alleged ASB with intensive support to help them address behavioural and other problems, with the overarching aim of breaking cycles of poor behaviour and bringing families back into mainstream housing. The model of provision employed was broadly based on the work of the Dundee Families Project (Dillane et al, 2001), in which families are provided with a range of services including some or all of the following:

- floating outreach support to family members in their existing home;
- outreach support in dispersed tenancies managed by the project;
- support in core residential accommodation managed by the project.

In practice, while the eight projects shared a number of common features, they had also developed a more nuanced and locally determined set of objectives and priorities.

While the overarching aim of FIPs is to enable families to change their lives and prevent eviction and homelessness, classifying projects as a form of either 'prevention' or 'early intervention' is problematic for a number of reasons. 'Prevention' usually refers to the provision of (often universal) strategies designed to reduce the likelihood of problems emerging, while 'early intervention' is most commonly understood as the provision of (targeted) activities on the basis of evidence of risk (Walker et al, 2007). Employing these definitions, FIPs cannot easily be located as a form of 'prevention' since they explicitly target families who are persistently the cause of complaints of ASB, with intervention only offered as a 'last resort' when other methods of addressing the problem behaviour are deemed to have failed. Equally, as this implies, projects rarely become involved with a family at the onset or 'early identification' of supposed 'risk factors'. In fact, we found that referral agencies more often viewed FIPs as a 'last chance' for families prior to the commencement of serious legal action (such as care or possession proceedings) or as a way of addressing gaps in social care service provision (Nixon et al, 2006a). It is therefore difficult to classify FIPs simply as a form of either 'prevention' or 'early intervention'.

Who do the projects target?

The government claims that the primary objective of FIPs is to change the behaviour of 'a small number of highly problematic families that account for a disproportionate amount of ASB' in order to 'restore safety to their homes and the wider community' (Home Office, 2006b, p 5). Our research has highlighted how families working with the eight FIPs were among the most deprived families in the country, with the vast majority living in 'hard-pressed' neighbourhoods where unemployment is high and incomes are low. Moreover, concerns about personal safety were defining factors in families' day-to-day lives, with many reporting that, as well as being the subject of complaints, they too had been victims of crime and ASB. Contrary to popular belief, rather than constituting a distinct minority distinguishable from the 'law-abiding majority', families tended to conform to the norms and values of the communities in which they lived (Nixon and Parr, 2008).

Both adults and children working with FIPs tended to have a high level of multiple support needs, which in many cases had not been adequately addressed by other agencies (Nixon et al, 2006a). For example, attention deficit hyperactivity disorder (ADHD) affected children in as many as one in five families compared to the national average, which predicts an incidence rate of between 3 and 8% of school-age children (Mytars, 2001; DCSF, 2005). Further, a wide range of health-related difficulties was prevalent among adult family members, with poor mental or physical health and/ or substance abuse affecting 80% of adults. Depression was the most widespread problem, affecting 59% of adults, with other mental health problems, such as schizophrenia, obsessive compulsive disorder, anxiety and stress affecting adults in a further fifth (21%) of families. For most families, alleged ASB was therefore only one symptom of a wider range of complex and interrelated patterns of disadvantage, with deprivation, ill-health, school exclusions and family breakdown all contributing to the marginalisation of family members. In this context of deep-rooted social exclusion and isolation, compounded by the debilitating impact of health-related problems, achieving change of any kind, let alone changes in parenting styles and behaviours, required a high degree of personal agency and strength.

What do FIPs do?

The specific services provided by FIPs fall into two distinct categories: the provision of direct work with children/adults, such as one-to-one support with parenting and family relationships, mentoring, formal/structured activities; and indirect work on behalf of children/adults involving liaison and referrals to other organisations. The level of involvement with family members' lives was very intense, with project workers seeking to help families unpick and analyse what needed to change in order for them to cease engaging in behaviour that led to complaints. While no single project model or 'blueprint' could be identified, there appeared to be a number of shared guiding principles that underpinned the approach adopted. For example, there was a strong emphasis on the employment of a multidisciplinary and multiagency focus embedded within local ASB partnerships; all the projects stressed equally the importance of intensive interventions sustained over a considerable length of time, with outreach support often required for over six months while residential support could continue for between one and two years. Project practices were clearly informed by the professional values of listening, being non-judgemental, promoting well-being and establishing relationships of trust.

Concerns about the behaviour of children commonly formed the key reason for families' referral to an FIP (Parr, 2007). In turn, children's/young people's troubled behaviour was often causally attributed to deficient parenting and a lack of household management skills. Thus, in their attempts to deal with the 'root causes' of ASB, a core aspect of project interventions focused on the development of strategies to assist parents/carers to increase their abilities to control their children's conduct. This was principally achieved through parenting skills training delivered via one-to-one sessions and/or courses run by external service providers. The general nature of the support provided to families was also aimed at assisting the parent/s to develop motivation and confidence to assert their role with their children. Moreover, the regular contact between project workers and families allowed project workers to play an active/practical role in helping families implement new household routines and parenting strategies, and facilitated parents' engagement with more formal courses. Although the guidance/training varied depending on the specific course and the age of the children/young people concerned, it commonly involved a mix of the following:

* setting clear household rules, routines and boundaries;
* developing the effective use of praise, incentives and rewards as a means to encourage cooperative behaviour;

- setting clear limits and following through with consequences;
- helping children to self-regulate their behaviour and understand the consequences of misbehaviour;
- encouraging play and family time with children;
- monitoring children and their whereabouts;
- managing misbehaviour effectively; and
- employing anger-management and calm-down strategies.

Such interventions met with varied success, and in the following section of the chapter we draw on families' accounts of the efficacy of parenting skills training, taking account of the diversity of provision, the varied modes of implementation and the specific family contexts.

Parenting interventions: what works, for whom and in what circumstances?

Talking to parents who had attended parenting courses/received one-to-one parenting guidance revealed a wide range of views on the effectiveness of such interventions. This may in part reflect differences in the quality and rigour of such courses, but it also seems to be associated with the 'problem' that parenting/guidance training was seeking to address. Many parents, particularly lone parents who were struggling to manage with few resources, were ready to acknowledge that they found it difficult to control their children's behaviour and were anxious to access support to enhance their ability to cope. As one mother explained:

> 'The kids had gone, they'd gone completely out of control, I couldn't control them no more. They wasn't listening to me, they was fighting, they was [coughs] being a general nuisance to everybody ... I was crying on the phone, 'I'm on drugs, I can't get off them, I'm trying so hard, I can't handle the kids' ... because the kids changed as well, obviously, because they knew that we wasn't fully aware of everything that was going on. So they was taking advantage and, I mean, we was letting them get away with it. There was no boundaries, there was no rules, there was nothing.' (Service user)

In this context, the provision of help with managing children's behaviours was welcomed, and many parents engaged willingly with the practical support provided and found it beneficial. Learning skills of 'active listening', the ability to negotiate in order to resolve conflict and avoiding entering into confrontational and upsetting arguments was particularly valued:

> 'To be quite honest, I've brought seven children up and I have found it very hard. But I took a lot on board from that [the parenting course] and achieved quite a lot, and I have achieved a lot more communication with me children, especially with me younger children.... There was one week where you listen and ask your child about

an incident and I found it really good with my three younger ones, mainly my youngest one. He goes to special school, and he were forever losing his rag and then walking out of school and that. I felt a bit silly first time I tried it, I did, I felt really silly ... and it did work really well and I use that quite a lot.' (Service user)

Outside 'formal' training sessions, 'support' around parenting and household skills often involved project staff visiting a family at key points during the day in order to encourage them to establish and adhere to routines, and to ensure that clear boundaries were in place. Some parents responded positively to such daily involvement in domestic life and welcomed the provision of additional support at what for them were difficult times of the day:

Q: 'And was that okay for you, you were sort of quite happy for her to come everyday?'

A: 'I weren't bothered because it were helping me, wasn't it, and if she didn't come he'd just stay in bed, wouldn't he? He weren't gonna go [to school]. "[Project worker's] coming," I goes, "You'd better get up, she's here in half an hour", and he got up before she come and got clothes on, so he knows.' (Service user)

For those who had gained from parenting interventions, the benefits went beyond help in addressing their children's troublesome behaviour. Where the form of FIP intervention was carefully and sensitively negotiated, some families reported that the provision of parenting training not only worked to assist them in managing disruptive behaviour, but also more generally helped improve family relations by encouraging parents to spend more time with their children, enjoy play and show affection. One mother explained how living in FIP core accommodation had enabled her to set boundaries and, as a result, her son's attitude towards her had changed dramatically. This mother concluded that she now had more confidence to deal with the generic difficulties associated with parenting teenagers:

'I mean, everyone should have it [parenting support], seriously, because teenagers – nobody can prepare you for teenagers. I'd lost my way. I mean, when I were bring them up on my own, I found them easier when they were younger. Don't get me wrong, but it's just when, for me, when they got to a certain age and they've got their own minds when they're teenagers and everything, and I just totally, I just lost the plot and with everything else that were happening, I mean, I didn't want to even live.' (Service user)

These strengthened family relations were perceived to have contributed to the long-term stabilisation of the family unit and in some cases were believed to have potentially reduced the risk of family breakdown:

> 'We're a family again. From being ripped and torn and, and scattered all about, we're back together … we feel more of a complete family now, we're doing family things together whereas we didn't before.' (Service user)

Additional benefits attributed to parenting classes included meeting people with similar problems and, more generally, socialising when otherwise a social life was problematic.

The intensity of FIP working practices allows support staff to play an active/practical role in implementing programmes of work – for example, around establishing and implementing daily routines and boundaries that enable individuals to change entrenched patterns of behaviour. The responsiveness of the project was viewed as practically and symbolically useful, with families affirming the value they placed on having a project worker on hand on a daily basis. This provided much-needed reassurance to families and gave adults, in particular, the support they needed to manage in times of crisis and where problems arose when implementing new methods of parenting or household routines that children resisted. The value of this type of support was seen as being particularly important in families where the mother was the subject of violent behaviour from teenage children (something that was common in a relatively high proportion of families referred to the projects), an issue that was often a hidden and unacknowledged source of conflict. This was, however, fundamentally dependent on the development of good and trusting relationships between project workers and service users.

As the above commentary illustrates, a number of families found parenting skills training useful and beneficial. For others, however, parenting skills training was deemed unsuccessful and/or unwarranted. As such, it is clear that parenting interventions are not a solution for all families. Perhaps not surprisingly, where parenting support is provided on a 'non-negotiable' basis, such as in core residential units, families can find daily visits by project staff and phone calls less a form of 'support' and more a programme of surveillance. For one interviewee, this was compounded by visits carried out by two project workers at a time. For this family, such contact was oppressive and had a detrimental effect on the mother, who stated that she had found the experience 'terrible'. Indeed, the relentlessness of the 'support' made her stressed and angry and served to add to the family's difficulties:

> 'I used to get quite mad and angry … because, oh, they were here just practically all [the] time and I were getting both of them together, which I didn't like…. It just didn't feel right, like two at once and things. So they were coming on a morning and then they were back at dinner and then later on at afternoon, and then were coming back at five to say goodnight. That were getting too much. I didn't like it … I did a lot of crying … they did try to say, you know, how they were there to support me and that … they were coming just to make sure everybody were up for school, everybody were getting ready, you know, for whatever.' (Service user)

In addition to the impact of project practices, when exploring why parenting interventions had met with negative responses, the age and the gender of children were also thought by many parents and other agencies to be relevant:

> 'I went on a couple of parenting courses, not that I thought they did any, any good ... I mean, they were just talking about setting out boundaries and things like that. Well it, it's hard when you've got a bloomin' 15-year-old lad.' (Service user)

One parent described how she had tried to adopt a rota for household tasks as recommended by her project worker but found that the time she spent badgering her teenage children to conform led to further arguments and conflict within the family. Despite the efforts of parents to develop new skills, the difficult behaviour presented by children was sometimes seen by parents as being beyond their control. Given the spectrum of reported behaviours of the children, this could reasonably be expected, despite intervention, as one mother explained:

> 'I think they [project] are actually trying everything aren't they ... giving me ideas on how to control them [three sons on ASBOs] and I do, I've phoned the police to breach them ... if they're not in [and] kicking off, smashing anything up I phone police straight away. So I do everything they tell me to do, it just doesn't always work.' (Service user)

Related to this, there was view among some parents that help with developing parenting skills was most effective when children were younger and when behaviour was less entrenched.

Beyond the general problems associated with parenting teenagers, for families with children who had pressing educational, social and behavioural needs, change was particularly difficult to achieve. These parents/carers were clear, therefore, that the parenting training and courses could not provide all the answers to their difficulties, recognising that there were no 'quick fixes' to the problems.

Adding to the complexity regarding the effects of parenting skills training was the way in which families conceptualised the 'problem' associated with their children's behaviour. Family intervention projects are based on a model of understanding that assumes that parenting is one of the most, if not *the* most, important underlying cause of ASB. In our research, although many parents acknowledged that they found it difficult to control their children's behaviour, the majority were also keenly resistant to the idea that their parenting was the cause of their children's disruptive behaviour and disputed the view that their children's behaviour was simply a reflection of their parenting abilities:

> 'I used to blame myself and then I thought, "Well no, why?" You know, me other two children are fine, you know, it's just, it's just a shame he's got in with a bad crowd. But I'm not, I'm not blaming myself for it. But I think that's a lot, what happens is, people

always, behind your back, "Oh she wants to learn to bring her kids up properly". You can't watch your kids 24/7.... They just think because they see he might be doing summat wrong, that we haven't brought our kids up properly.' (Service user)

Linear associations commonly made in popular and professional discourses between poor parenting and children's behaviour were therefore the cause of frustration for many. In defence, a number of parents explained how they had taken action to address the ASB displayed by their children and were keen to convey how they monitored their children's behaviour and intervened when necessary.

'But it's not, it's not as though, I said, I keep saying to Steven, "Do you know, they're making out as though we're bad parents and we're not". We do care but, and they're not out, they're in at a decent time every night.' (Service user)

As the above excerpt from an interview with a mother illustrates, some people resented the implication that their parenting was deficient and did not feel they needed to attend a parenting programme. Equally, where children suffered from depression and other forms of mental health conditions and/or where children had special educational needs, parents often felt that they were unfairly being held culpable for behaviour that they could do little to change without further specialist support. Commonly, parents had found it difficult to get agencies to recognise the severity of mental health conditions and described feelings of exacerbation and despair at the debilitating effects of trying to manage their children's very difficult and challenging behaviour:

'And it is scary. I mean, I hold me hands up. I try not to show it, but I am scared when she gets into that rage, definitely.' (Service user)

A theme evident across parents' accounts was a resistance to what may be viewed as a discourse of blame, and for some families the projects' intervention in their personal and domestic life was experienced as unnecessary, intrusive and unwelcome.

Discussion and conclusion

The evidence in relation to the efficacy of parenting programmes suggests that, while some parents welcomed the provision of such interventions and found them to have been successful in helping them achieve positive change, they were not a solution for all families. A number of parents resisted the imposition of parenting skills training and/or reported that the techniques promoted in parenting courses did not work for them. This demonstrates how the success or failure of parenting skills training is contingent on the context in which the guidance/training is offered. The research findings suggest that there is a wide range of factors likely to affect whether or not parenting interventions 'work', including:

- the seriousness of the behaviour concerned;
- whether the family has been compelled to attend a parenting course or is engaging voluntarily;
- the age and gender of the child(ren);
- whether contextual factors – personal, familial or social – are likely to negate the impact of parenting skills training; and
- the extent to which parenting/household guidance is delivered in a sensitive manner that is responsive to the needs of the family.

Among other things, these findings draw attention to the important role that professional habitus – 'the cultural, emotional and instrumental repertoires and dispositions for cognition and action' (Stenson, 2005, p 274) – play in the implementation and 'success' of parenting skills training. The fact that some families actively resist the notion that they require parenting skills training highlights how important it is for project workers to take account of families' views of their needs and the cause of children's problem behaviour. Where project workers are unresponsive, engagement with parenting support is not only likely to be less productive, but also risks having a detrimental impact on already-fragile families. At the very least, FIPs need to ensure that they do not place additional pressures on already vulnerable families.

Moreover, as well as taking into account the different factors that might inhibit or promote 'success', we would argue that further attention needs to be paid to the provision of parenting training as a blanket provision for all families working with FIPs. While we would not deny that in some families parents are struggling to care for children and young people, it is not necessarily the case that all families require, and should be compelled to attend, parenting training. Rather, we would suggest that decisions about whether parenting support is deemed to be a valuable and positive intervention should be based on parental choice combined with robust assessment procedures. It is important that staff are skilled in assessing the complex causes of problematic behaviour and the role of poor parenting skills within this. This brings into focus the importance of staff experience and training. The different ways adult and/or children's problematic behaviour might be understood, the models of assessment utilised and methods of support employed will vary depending on the professional identities of the staff employed. Decisions about the necessity of parenting skills training also requires being attentive to unreflective attempts to impose moral judgements on what are perceived to be disorderly household and domestic routines. Holt (2008) identifies how discourses and practices that surround parenting interventions draw on classifications of practices based on white, nuclear family parenting norms. Further, it is acknowledged that most parenting support programmes derive from a set of distinctly middle-class values that do not automatically recognise different cultural attitudes towards childrearing practices (Ghate and Ramella, 2002; Katz et al, 2007; Moran et al, 2008). Such values not only tend to position working-class mothers within a paradigm of 'parenting deficit' but, as Goldson and Jamieson (2002, p 94) highlight, the failure to contextualise responses can result in a devaluing of 'working class culture and values in which practices are analysed in a "dematerialised and decontextualised" form, separating it from critical questions of political economy, ignoring the primary concept of social justice and emphasising the imperative of control'. Such observations reinforce the need identified by Gillies (2005) to engage in vital normative questions about the purpose of parenting skills training and who really benefits.

To conclude, in common with other commentators who call for a more nuanced analysis and understanding of the impact of Parenting Orders, our research into FIPs' use of parenting interventions suggests that such practices should not be judged on a simplistic dichotomous paradigm of 'good' or 'bad' but rather should be understood as a complex and contradictory site in which regulation and coercion sit side by side with opportunities for difficulties to be recognised and practical support provided (Holt, 2008, p 213). Such discontinuities are important since they may provide a critical opportunity for resistance, subversion and the exercise of personal agency.

Notes

[1] By April 2008, more than 60 FIPs had been established with funding from the now defunct Respect Taskforce.

[2] For a discussion of the gendered nature of anti-social behaviour (ASB) interventions, see Nixon and Hunter (2009: forthcoming).

References

Cabinet Office (2008) *Whole family approaches*, London: Cabinet Office.
DCSF (Department for Children, Schools and Families) (2005) *Every child matters: Outcomes framework*, London: DCSF (www.everychildmatters.gov.uk).
DCSF (2008) *Youth taskforce action plan: Give respect, get respect*, London: DFCS.
Dillane, J., Hill, M., Bannister, J. and Scott, S. (2001) *Evaluation of the Dundee Families Project*, Edinburgh: Scottish Executive.
Ghate, D. and Ramella, M. (2002) *Positive parenting: The national evaluation of the Youth Justice Board's Parenting Programme*, London: Programme Policy Research Bureau.
Gillies, V. (2005) 'Meeting parents' needs? Discourses of "support" and "inclusion" in family policy', *Critical Social Policy*, vol 25, no 1, pp 70-90.
Goldson, B. and Jamieson, J. (2002) 'Youth crime, the "parenting deficit" and state intervention: a contextual critique', *Youth Justice*, vol 2, no 2, pp 82-99.
Holt, A. (2008) 'Room for resistance? Parenting Orders, disciplinary power and the production of the "bad parent"', in P. Squires (ed) *ASBO nation: The criminalisation of nuisance*, Bristol: The Policy Press.
Home Office (2006a) *Respect action plan*, London: Home Office.
Home Office (2006b) *Family intervention projects: Respect guide*, London: Home Office.

Jones, A., Pleace, N., Quillgars, D. and Sanderson, D. (2005) *Shelter Inclusion Project: Evaluation of a new model to address anti-social behaviour*, York: Centre for Housing Policy, University of York.

Katz, I., Corylan, J., La Place, B. and Hunter, S. (2007) *The relationship between parenting and poverty*, York: Joseph Rowntree Foundation, www.jrf.org.uk/bookshop/ebooks/parenting-poverty.pdf

Lister, D. (2006) 'Children (but not women) first: New Labour, child welfare and gender', *Critical Social Policy*, vol 26, no 2, pp 315-35.

Moran, P., Ghate, D. and Van der Merwe, A. (2008) *What works in parenting support: A review of the evidence*, Policy Research Bureau, Research Report RR574, London: DfES, www.prb.org.uk/wwiparenting/RR574.pdf

Mytars, D. (2001) 'Understanding and recognizing ADHD', *Practice Nursing*, vol 21, no 7, pp 278-80.

Nixon, J. and Hunter, C. (2009: forthcoming) 'Discipline women: ASB and the governance of conduct', in A. Millie (ed) *Securing respect: Behavioural expectations and anti-social behaviour in the UK*, Bristol: The Policy Press.

Nixon, J. and Parr, S. (2008) *The longer term outcomes associated with families who had worked with intensive family support projects 2004 - 2006/7*, Housing Research Summary 240, London: Department for Communities and Local Government.

Nixon, J., Hunter, C., Parr, S., Whittle, S., Myers, S. and Sanderson, D. (2006a) *Interim evaluation of rehabilitation projects for families at risk of losing their home as a result of ASB*, London: ODPM.

Nixon, J., Hunter, C., Parr, S., Whittle, S., Myers, S. and Sanderson, D. (2006b) *ASB intensive family support projects: An evaluation of 6 pioneering projects*, London: DCLG.

Parr, S. (2007) *The Leeds Signpost Family Intervention Project: An evaluation*, Sheffield: CRESR, Sheffield Hallam University.

Parr, S. (2008) 'Family intervention projects: a site of social work practice', *British Journal of Social Work*, Advance access, 29 April, doi:10.1093/bjsw/bcn057.

Parr, S. and Nixon, J. (2008) 'Rationalising family intervention projects', in P. Squires (ed) *ASBO nation: The criminalisation of nuisance*, Bristol: The Policy Press.

Parr, S., Nixon, J. and Duffy, D. (2008) *The Wakefield Family First Project: An evaluation*, Sheffield: Centre for Regional and Economic Social Research, Sheffield Hallam University.

Stenson, K. (2005) 'Sovereignty, biopolitics and local government of crime in England', *Theoretical Criminology*, vol 9, no 3, pp 265-87.

Walker, J., Thompson, C., Laing, K., Raybould, S., Coombes, M., Procter, S. and Wren, C. (2007) *Youth Inclusion and Support Panels: Preventing crime and anti-social behaviour?*, London: DCSF.

4

Early intervention and prevention: lessons from the Sure Start programme

Karen Clarke

Introduction

The concept of social exclusion has been central to New Labour's social policy since its election in 1997. Shortly after its election success, the government announced the setting up of the Social Exclusion Unit, located in the Cabinet Office, working with the Number 10 Policy Unit and reporting to the Prime Minister (Levitas, 2005, p 147). The unit was staffed by co-opted members from the civil service, the police, the voluntary sector and business, and involved government ministers from across a range of government departments, reflecting the way in which social exclusion was understood as involving multiple causes and resulting in a range of social problems.

An important feature of the conceptualisation of social exclusion is its intergenerational reproduction: longitudinal social surveys indicate that children born to parents who are socially excluded are themselves at much greater risk of being socially excluded themselves as they grow up (Welshman, 2007). This has resulted in a central place being given to policies that aim to intervene to prevent it. Seeing the process of social exclusion in terms of a cycle of disadvantage or of deprivation has in turn resulted in a focus on the significance of early childhood experience and an unprecedented expansion of policies and services directed at preschool children and their parents. The Sure Start programme, announced in 1998 and expanded by 2004 to include 400,000 children under four and their families, has been a central element in the government's long-term strategy to prevent social exclusion by breaking the cycle that plays a significant part in its (re)production. This chapter looks at how the problem of the intergenerational reproduction of social exclusion has been conceptualised by the New Labour governments and how this is reflected in policy. It examines the evolving policy interventions since 1997 with parents of preschool children designed to 'break the cycle', and what this conceptualisation of social exclusion and the policies associated with it leave out.

Social exclusion and its reproduction

The concept of social exclusion is a complex one, with numerous overlapping definitions. A report by Ruth Levitas and colleagues at the University of Bristol for the Social Exclusion Unit identified 12 different definitions of social exclusion/inclusion in use by different government departments, by academics and within the European Union. These definitions operate at different levels, are normative to different extents and are operationalised using a variety of different indicators. Definitions often do not distinguish clearly between the causes of social exclusion, identified as 'risk factors', and the effects or outcomes of social exclusion (Levitas et al, 2007).

As earlier work by Levitas (2005) has shown, 'social exclusion' is used in different ways in three different discourses, which offer different implicit understandings of the processes that lead to social exclusion (and therefore of the policies that are needed to address the problem). The redistributionist discourse attributes social exclusion to inequalities in the social structure, and under this conceptualisation the problem requires the redistribution of resources to those who are socially excluded. Within the social inclusionist discourse, which Levitas argues is the dominant discourse for New Labour, the rights and responsibilities of citizenship stem primarily from paid employment, and therefore paid work offers the most effective and appropriate route out of social exclusion, with the role of the state being to ensure as far as possible that opportunities for employment are made available to all. In a third discourse, the moral underclass discourse, social exclusion is a consequence of individual moral failings, stemming at least in part from the sometimes perverse incentives offered by the structure of welfare systems. The solution to social exclusion understood in this way lies in the transformation of the values and culture of those who are socially excluded, coupled with the removal, where possible, of perverse incentives. The ambiguity of the concept of social exclusion allows discourse to slide imperceptibly from one discourse to another. In particular, Levitas argues, the social inclusionist discourse shifts easily into a moral underclass discourse. This seems to be borne out in the development of policies aimed at preventing social exclusion through interventions with young children and their parents, in which the social inclusionist and moral underclass discourses are dominant, and the redistributionist discourse relatively neglected (Clarke, 2006, 2007).

The Social Exclusion Task Force (set up in 2006 to replace the Social Exclusion Unit, originally established in December 1997) gives the following definition of social exclusion:

> It is a short-hand term for what can happen when people or areas have a combination of linked problems, such as unemployment, discrimination, poor skills, low incomes, poor housing, high crime and family breakdown. These problems are linked and mutually reinforcing. Social exclusion is an extreme consequence of what happens when people don't get a fair deal throughout their lives, often because of disadvantage they face at birth, and this disadvantage can be transmitted from one generation to

the next. (Social Exclusion Task Force website, www.cabinetoffice.gov.uk/social_
exclusion_task_force/context.aspx)

The key features of this definition are that social exclusion:

- is an attribute of both individuals and areas;
- has a number of different dimensions that involve both individual and family/
household characteristics (poor skills, family breakdown, low income) and
environmental characteristics (poor housing, discrimination, unemployment
and high crime) and some dimensions that are ambiguous across individuals,
households and environment (unemployment, high crime);
- results from the interaction of these different dimensions/characteristics; and
- is a process occurring over time and across generations.

Consistent with the dominant social integrationist discourse on social exclusion, the
principal focus of New Labour's policies was initially on paid work as the best route
out of poverty and social exclusion. A number of welfare reforms were introduced
that provided a combination of 'sticks' and 'carrots' to reduce unemployment and to
make paid employment financially worthwhile. One of the particular target groups for
these policies was parents. The New Deal for Lone Parents provided encouragement,
advice and support for lone parents to enter the labour market. The Working Families'
Tax Credit (subsequently extended to non-parents as the Working Tax Credit) and
the Childcare Tax Credit, combined with policies to expand childcare and nursery
education, sought to address the availability and cost of childcare for working parents.
The Child Tax Credit and an increase in Child Benefit gave all parents, but particularly
those at the lower end of the income distribution, significant increases in income.

Although the redistributionist discourse of social exclusion, emphasising poverty and
material inequality, has been relatively unimportant within New Labour's policies to
address social exclusion, there has been an exception in the case of child poverty.
Child poverty and the long-term effects of growing up in poverty were identified as
problems of particular importance relatively early in the first New Labour government.
In 1999, Tony Blair made his historic commitment to eradicate child poverty 'in a
generation', that is, by 2020, with milestones towards this target identified for 2004-
05 (25% reduction) and 2010 (50% reduction) to mark the route to its eventual
achievement. A key aspect of the long-term strategy for reducing child poverty
has been intervening in what is seen to be the cyclical processes involved in social
exclusion to prevent the children of socially excluded parents from becoming socially
excluded themselves. The Sure Start programme was introduced as the means for
intervening to interrupt the cycle of deprivation or disadvantage.

Sure Start and early intervention

The Sure Start programme emerged from the cross-departmental review of services
for children under eight, which was part of the first Comprehensive Spending Review

carried out in 1997 (Glass, 1999). The focus of the cross-departmental review was on young children and social exclusion with the aim of identifying what policies and services were needed at a family and community level 'to ensure the development of their full potential throughout their lives' (Glass, 1999, p 260). Although the initial brief was to look at services for children under eight, this was modified to focus on children under four as it became clear that the greatest problems in service provision lay in the early years and also because the accumulated evidence suggested that 'successful intervention in the earliest years offered the greatest potential for making a difference' (Glass, 1999, p 260).

As part of the review, a series of seminars was held, involving academics, policy makers and representatives from the voluntary sector, at which evidence was presented, drawn from a number of longitudinal cohort studies, demonstrating an association between a number of variables taken as indicators of, and risk factors for, social exclusion (low birthweight, developmental delay, poor health, teenage pregnancy, poor parenting, school exclusion, criminal activity and many more) (see, for example, Pugh, 1998, p 10), and a variety of later adverse outcomes that overlap with the causes of exclusion (for example, teenage pregnancy, juvenile offending, poor educational achievement and adult unemployment). The aim of Sure Start was:

> to work with parents-to-be, parents and children to promote the physical, intellectual and social development of babies and young children – particularly those who are disadvantaged – so that they can flourish at home and when they get to school, and thereby break the cycle of disadvantage for the current generation of young children. (Sure Start, 2002, p 19)

As its name implies, the programme drew on the model of Head Start and other US early intervention programmes such as the Perry/High Scope programme. Head Start was developed in the US in the 1960s as part of the War on Poverty, and provided preschool experience for four- and five-year-olds from poor families to enable them to start school on a more equal footing with their better-off peers. Evidence presented at the Treasury seminars drew attention to the long-term financial savings that this 'investment' in services for young children could generate (Clarke, 2006).

The initial announcement in 1998 was for a programme of 250 Sure Start Local Programmes (SSLPs) in areas of high deprivation, covering 187,000 children under four (about 18% of the total population of poor children in the age group) to be rolled out between 1999 and 2002. In 2000 the Treasury announced that the size of the programme was to be doubled to cover 400,000 children in over 500 SSLPs. Each SSLP had a clearly defined catchment area, serving the population of children under four and their parents, living within 'pram-pushing' distance of the services offered. The programme was intended to be delivered in a way that was not stigmatising: within the Sure Start area, services were available to all families with a child under four. It was also intended to empower parents and to develop services that reflected locally identified needs. To this end, parents were to be involved in all levels of governance of the SSLPs. The intention was that Sure Start should provide services covering a range of interlinked family needs, including health, education and family support, with outreach work providing support to parents at home where necessary. The guidance issued to SSLPs outlined the core services that were to be provided:

- outreach and home visiting;
- support for families and parents;
- support for good-quality play, learning and childcare experiences for children;
- primary and community healthcare and advice about child health and development and family health; and
- support for people with special needs, including help accessing specialised services (Melhuish and Hall, 2007, pp 13-14).

Within this broad framework the SSLPs were free to develop services and methods of delivery in whatever way they judged most appropriate. There was therefore no 'blueprint' for Sure Start and, as an area-based initiative, its focus, at least in theory, was on whole communities rather than individual families. These features distinguish Sure Start from the US programmes such as Head Start and other similar preschool intervention projects, which provided the evidence used to justify the programme. The US programmes were delivered to individual families who enrolled on them, rather than being universally available to all families in a given area, and, unlike Sure Start, they followed a specific protocol for delivery. The quality and effectiveness of SSLPs were controlled through setting targets for the outcomes to be achieved, in the form of Public Service Agreements, leaving the means for achieving these targets to be determined locally. The targets set for Sure Start transformed complex research evidence into a set of measurable outcomes that promoted a view of mothers as principally responsible for children's development and well-being, and which risked sliding into a moral underclass discourse of social exclusion that blames parents, in particular mothers, for poor outcomes (Clarke, 2006). This perspective is arguably also reflected in the national evaluation of the outcomes of Sure Start.

Outcomes and lessons

Consistent with New Labour's emphasis on evidence-based policy and a concern to establish 'what works', the Sure Start programme included a requirement that each of the SSLPs established its own evaluation, and a large-scale national evaluation programme was also commissioned from a team of researchers at Birkbeck College. A total of £20 million has been spent on the evaluation programme (Ward, 2005).

The national evaluation faced substantial design difficulties because of the variability between SSLPs in the services introduced, the variation in leadership and governance arrangements, the heterogeneity of areas in which the programme was set up and the absence of suitable 'controls' against which to compare outcomes (Rutter, 2007). So far, two reports looking at the outcomes of the programme have been produced.

The first was published in late 2005 and the second in March 2008 (NESS, 2005, 2008).

The first report compared outcomes in the first 150 SSLPs with 50 similarly disadvantaged areas that had been selected to have a SSLP but had not yet begun to implement it. The study looked at outcomes for children at nine months and at 36 months and also examined various aspects of parenting and maternal well-being (Belsky and Melhuish, 2007). The findings were disappointing. While there had been some modest benefits for some children in SSLP areas, there were adverse effects for others. Perhaps most worryingly, the adverse effects were suffered by those children and families who were most disadvantaged: lone mothers, young mothers and workless households.

The only differences in parenting in SSLP areas and non-SSLP areas that were statistically significant were:

- Households of nine-month-olds in Sure Start areas were less chaotic than those of nine-month-olds in the comparator areas;
- The mothers of 36-month-olds were more accepting of their children; and
- Non-teenage mothers showed less negative parenting.

However, overall, there was little difference in parenting between SSLP areas and non-SSLP areas (Belsky and Melhuish, 2007).

In terms of child outcomes there were no significant effects evident for the nine-month-olds. The three-year-old children of non-teenage mothers in SSLP areas had fewer behaviour problems and scored more highly in terms of social competence than the non-SSLP comparators. However, the children of teenage mothers in SSLP areas had lower verbal ability and a higher level of behaviour problems than those in the non-SSLP areas. Three-year-olds in workless households and in lone-parent families in the SSLP areas also scored lower than their non-SSLP counterparts in terms of verbal ability.

These findings were interpreted as showing that the better-off families in poor areas were better at accessing the services provided and that they had in a sense 'crowded out' the more socially excluded families in the area. The way in which these findings appear to have influenced the direction of subsequent policy on social exclusion will be discussed further below.

The findings presented in the second national evaluation report on the outcomes of Sure Start were more positive (NESS, 2008). The study looked at a range of outcomes for three-year-olds living in the 150 longest-running SSLPs compared with a sample of children and their parents from the Millennium Cohort Study who lived in similarly deprived areas that did not have an SSLP in 2003-04. For seven out of 14 indicators selected by the evaluators, there were positive effects in SSLP areas relating to child health, children's social behaviour and competence, and the quality of parenting. Furthermore, the negative outcomes for some three-year-olds living in Sure Start areas that were reported in 2005 were not found in the 2008 report.

The differences in outcomes between SSLP and non-SSLP areas for children were as follows:

- *Child health:* children living in SSLP areas were more likely to have had all the recommended immunisations by age three and were less likely to have had an accident for which medical attention had been sought. However, further analysis suggested that these differences between SSLP areas and non-SSLP areas may have been a consequence of the timing of the data collection for the two groups.
- *Child behaviour:* children in SSLP areas had higher average scores for positive social behaviour and for independence/self-regulation.

There was no significant difference between SSLP and non-SSLP areas in parents' rating of children's negative social behaviour or in children's cognitive and language development measured through a picture naming task.

In relation to parenting, the differences between SSLP and non-SSLP areas that were statistically significant were:

- Problematic parenting, as measured by the Parenting Risk Index, was lower on average in families in SSLP areas.
- The Home Learning Environment score was higher on average in SSLP areas.

There was no difference between the two groups in father involvement.

Scoring for almost all these variables was based on maternal reports, combined with interviewer observation in two sub-areas within the Parenting Risk Index. The evaluation team commented that it would have been desirable to have been able to examine outcomes on bases other than maternal reports (NESS, 2008).

Further analysis indicated that the positive outcomes for children were a consequence of better parenting and home environment scores.

The final difference to emerge between SSLP and non-SSLP areas was that families in SSLP areas had made use of more different types of support than those in non-SSLP areas. Presumably, this may reflect differences between areas in the availability of services, as well as in parental willingness to make use of the services that were available.

Variables for which there were no significant differences between parents in SSLP and non-SSLP areas were maternal well-being (smoking, life satisfaction and body mass index) and mother's rating of the area in which she lived.

Unlike the findings from the earlier evaluation, there was no evidence of negative effects for the most disadvantaged subgroups living in the Sure Start areas. The authors suggest that by the time the second outcomes study took place, the SSLPs were more securely established, and were therefore more likely to be reaching all families in the area, rather than just being accessed by the least disadvantaged. For the three-year-olds in the more recent evaluation study, the SSLP had been in existence for the whole of their first three years and there had therefore been an opportunity for families to access services and support for the whole period of early childhood. The evidence presented is interpreted cautiously but seems to indicate that there have been modest improvements in children's social behaviour at age three, which seems to be explained by more positive mothering in Sure Start areas.

The developing conceptualisation of social exclusion and policy consequences

The publication of the *Every child matters* Green Paper in 2003 (HM Treasury, 2003) is a landmark in the development of New Labour's policies to address social exclusion by early intervention. The Green Paper covered services for children aged 0 to 19 and placed parents at the centre of these policies. Parents were to be supported by a range of services provided by agencies working in partnership under an integrated Children and Young People's Plan (Parton, 2006; Churchill, 2007). The report refers to the government's intention 'to put supporting parents and carers at the heart of its approach to improving children's lives', on the grounds that 'the bond between the child and their parents is the most critical influence on a child's life' (HM Treasury, 2003, p 39). It identifies a range of universal and targeted services for parents and carers, with compulsion for parents who fail to meet their responsibilities. The emphasis on prevention and early intervention gives a key role to the identification of those individuals and families who are at greatest risk of social exclusion, in order to target resources most effectively. This in turn has involved the government in further refining the concept of social exclusion, with important implications for preventative welfare policies.

In a speech originally given to the Centre for the Analysis of Social Exclusion, reviewing progress on reducing social exclusion, David Miliband (2006), then Minister of Communities and Local Government, differentiated social exclusion into three subcategories: 'wide', 'deep' and 'concentrated' social exclusion. Those included in the category of wide social exclusion are 'the large minority of people' who 'lack the things most people take for granted': 'basic skills, a job, a decent home, a sufficient income, and contact with friends and family' (Miliband, 2006, p 6). Miliband identified the category of deep social exclusion as including those who suffer five or more out of 10 disadvantages:

- unemployment;
- living in a workless household;
- having no educational qualifications;
- living in social housing;
- living in overcrowded conditions;
- suffering poor mental health;
- suffering poor health;
- living alone;
- lacking consumer durables; or
- enduring financial stress (Miliband, 2006, p 7).

These, he argues, are a group who are more recognisably socially excluded. The third category – concentrated social exclusion – refers to the geographical concentration of disadvantage.

Miliband argued for the need to set appropriate mainstream performance targets for government departments and for services that would provide an appropriate 'floor' for the most disadvantaged (both areas and individuals) as a way of mainstreaming services and avoiding the stigma associated with special interventions with the most highly disadvantaged. He argued for the importance of prevention, conceptualised as 'investment' rather than 'crisis' intervention, as the most cost-effective form of public expenditure. His discussion is couched in highly instrumental, social investment terms. He identifies the task of government as being to assess 'where in the lifecycle the biggest returns exist – whether to continue to invest more in children and early years, or spread money more evenly across the life cycle' (Miliband, 2006, p 11). However, his focus on mainstreaming services and avoiding special interventions that might be stigmatising is important and consistent with the ideas that informed the setting up of Sure Start. There are hints at the same time of a moral underclass discourse of social exclusion in Miliband's reference to the need to ensure that citizens 'are motivated to learn or work, adopt healthier diets and exercise, and adhere to standards of behaviour' (Miliband, 2006, p 11).

The (re)appearance of the problem family

The concept of the deeply socially excluded recurs in the report of the Social Exclusion Task Force (2006) entitled *Reaching out: An action plan on social exclusion*, which presents the government's action plan on social exclusion. Here, however, the need to retain a universal and non-stigmatising approach seems to have disappeared. The report identifies a small minority of families who suffer 'persistent and deep-seated exclusion', with signs of disadvantage that 'appear early in life and persist long into adulthood' (2006, p 13). By drawing on international evidence for the existence of such a group, the report appears to imply that such deep social exclusion is not a result of the context in which such families live, or produced under particular social circumstances, but rather is a consequence of the inherent characteristics of the individuals who make up such families. It refers to 'international evidence [which] shows that around 2.7 per cent of 15-year-olds … can be described as having multiple problems' and later to 'longitudinal evidence from New Zealand [which] shows that … for children born to the 5 per cent most disadvantaged families, more than 216 in 1000 will end up with multiple problems at 15' (pp 17-18).

Tony Blair, in a speech to the Joseph Rowntree Foundation coinciding with the publication of the Social Exclusion Task Force report, identified a similar percentage of the population in Britain when he said: 'About 2.5 per cent of every generation seem to be stuck in a life-time of disadvantage and amongst them are the excluded of the excluded, the deeply excluded' (Blair, 2006). He identified such families as falling into a different category from poor families more generally: 'The answer for these families is that a rising tide of material prosperity will not necessarily raise all ships'. He argued that their problems were 'about their social and human capital as much as financial' (Blair, 2006). Similarly, the Social Exclusion Task Force report talked about families 'caught in the deepest cycles of deprivation and disadvantage' who face barriers that are 'not only economic but also social and cultural' and for whom New Labour's programmes had produced only modest results (Social Exclusion Task Force, 2006, p 20). In both cases, there is an implicit moral underclass discourse of social exclusion, which sees the socially excluded as characterised by different social and cultural values from the rest of society.

Blair's speech constructs such families as 'other' by presenting a contrast between 'normal families' and intervention in 'a dysfunctional family', which does not engage with universal services, either because it does not want to or does not know how to. While normal families will engage with universal services of their own accord, the implication of the Social Exclusion Task Force report's title, and of the policies that have followed from it, is that deeply excluded families have to be actively engaged by the state. Such families are to be specifically targeted for intensive and special intervention. The discourse here is reminiscent of that relating to 'problem families', who were the subject of intensive preventive family casework in the 1950s and 1960s. Parton (2006, p 22) describes how it was assumed that 'growing affluence and employment and reduced poverty meant that such problems were small scale and primarily located in a small number of "problem families"'. A similar analysis seems to be appearing for England in the early 21st century.

A shift in the policy approach to social exclusion is signalled in *Reaching out* and the two reports that have followed it (Social Exclusion Task Force, 2007a, 2008): 'Addressing these issues means a significant change in the way central and local government address social exclusion' (Social Exclusion Task Force, 2007b, p 8). The shift involves identifying the 'deeply disadvantaged' and focusing a range of services on them, with aims that are simultaneously addressing current problems and preventing future ones, and which offer services for all members of the family. The holistic, family approach is reflected in the use of the phrase 'think family' in the titles of two subsequent reports from the Social Exclusion Task Force (2007a, 2008). Unlike the universal approach taken by Sure Start, where the aim was to address what would in the new terminology be identified as wide and concentrated social exclusion, the emphasis now is focused on deep exclusion and the identification and separation from the rest of the population of this problem minority. By targeting families rather than geographical areas, the problem becomes located in the family rather than in the social and physical environment in which the family lives.

The Action Plan on Social Exclusion draws on research evidence as the basis for proposing that it is possible to identify risks associated with specific outcomes and consequently to 'accurately target supportive interventions at high-risk groups' (Social Exclusion Task Force, 2006, p 26). This makes the collection of data on individuals and families a crucial activity, which the report states 'can easily be captured or collated by those on the front line and in contact with vulnerable individuals' (p 27). Resistance to engagement with preventative services is to be countered by 'a redoubling of efforts to engage – persistence with personalisation' (p 28). In this context, the problem of social exclusion seems to be increasingly equated with offending behaviour.

The shift to addressing social exclusion through identifying and working with a small minority of the deeply excluded has been accompanied by an increasing preference for delivery of professionally developed and evidence-based programmes, drawing primarily on work done in the US. Within this approach there is little room for the identification of need by those for whom the services are intended, or for user involvement in the governance of the programme, which was one of the principles that informed Sure Start. Because such interventions are based on the identification of at-risk groups, rather than areas, neighbourhoods or communities, there is less scope for involving those who are targeted by the programme in its management.

An example of this, relevant to the focus of Sure Start on families with preschool children, is the piloting of an intervention with young pregnant women in 10 areas in England, using a programme developed by David Olds in the US and delivered by specially trained midwives (Social Exclusion Task Force, 2006). The Nurse–Family Partnership programme was evaluated in the US using a randomised controlled trial (RCT) design and was established in England in March 2007 as the Family Nurse Partnership (FNP). The aims of the programme are to improve pregnancy outcome, to improve child health and development and to improve parents' economic self-sufficiency. It has been piloted initially in 10 areas, with a further 20 areas to join from 2008. The tender document for local authorities bidding for the programme extension describes the FNP as follows:

> The FNP is an intensive preventive home visiting programme delivered by specially trained nurses and midwives who have experience of working with families in the community. It is a structured programme offered to at risk, first time young parents

> from early pregnancy until the child is 2 years old. Pregnancy and birth are key points when most families are highly receptive to support and extra help. (DCSF, 2008, p 1)

The FNP works with first-time mothers under the age of 20, delivering a tightly prescribed programme that specifies the average time to be allocated within visits during pregnancy and in the child's first two years to each of five 'domains': personal health, maternal role, family and friends, environmental health and life course development. It specifies that 10 to 15% of each visit on average is to be devoted to family and friends during pregnancy, infancy and toddlerhood; personal health is to be covered in 35 to 40% of the visit time in pregnancy, 14 to 20% of the time in infancy and 10 to 15% in toddlerhood. Programme fidelity is stressed as extremely important, although there is acknowledgement of the 'creative tension' between fidelity to the programme and responding to the specific circumstances of each family (DCSF, 2008). A programme of this kind seems to allow relatively little space for women to identify their own needs and develop agency and autonomy. Although there is reference when describing the aims of the programme to developing economic self-sufficiency, it is not clear how and where this is meant to come into the programme and what the role of midwives is in promoting this.

Sure Start and the transformation into children's centres

At the same time as the approach to social exclusion has shifted towards a narrow focus on a particular subset of the socially excluded, Sure Start has undergone a transformation in the direction of greater universality. The 10-year strategy for childcare published in 2004 (HM Treasury, 2004, p 1) announced the setting up of children's centres in every community to provide all families with 'easy access to integrated services', 'offering information, health, family support, childcare and other services for parents and children'. The proposals were presented in the context of offering parents 'choice about how to balance work and family life', and appear to be primarily focused on supporting and facilitating parental employment, but with the aim of 'giving every child the best start in life' (HM Treasury, 2004, p 1).

On the one hand, this policy announcement was a welcome recognition of the importance of early years services, which would make them universally available. On the other, Norman Glass, the Treasury civil servant who played a key role in the setting up of Sure Start, saw it as the abolition of Sure Start, and its replacement by a 'New Deal for Toddlers' focused on getting parents into paid work. Glass anticipated that, as children's centres all came under local authority control, they would lose their local ownership by parents and those working on the programme. Furthermore, he predicted that their level of funding would be severely cut back to enable the setting up of a much larger number of children's centres, with the abolition of ring-fenced funding further threatening the resources available for preschool children and their parents (Glass, 2005). If Glass's analysis is correct, the transition from SSLPs to Sure

Start children's centres represents the dominance in this context of an approach to social exclusion very much within the social inclusionist discourse framework, in which paid employment offers the route to social inclusion.

Conclusions

This chapter has examined the relationship between New Labour's policies for early intervention to prevent social exclusion and its evolving conceptualisation of what social exclusion is and what causes it. Sure Start was introduced early in New Labour's first term of government as a central element in the long-term strategy to address social exclusion that sought to intervene in the processes that were seen to result in its reproduction from one generation to the next. Its objective of ensuring that children reached school 'ready to learn' was consistent with an approach to reducing social exclusion through paid work. The aim was to ensure that children from socially excluded families did not start school at a disadvantage and that they were therefore able to benefit equally from the opportunities to gain qualifications that would give them a secure place in the labour market in adulthood. The means for achieving this, at least as reflected in the national targets for Sure Start and in the outcomes examined in the national evaluation, are focused on issues that veer towards a moral underclass conceptualisation of social exclusion. There is a strong emphasis on modifying maternal behaviour to reflect a particular middle-class set of family values, with children's attainment and behaviour examined exclusively in terms of the 'parenting' (for which read 'mothering') they receive. Material poverty as an explanation of social exclusion disappears in the evaluation of outcomes, as something to be controlled for, and therefore effectively ignored.

The tensions in the concept of social exclusion between its use in a social inclusionist and in a moral underclass discourse have been resolved as policy has evolved during New Labour's second and third terms. The government's policies to reduce social exclusion are located more firmly in one or the other perspective. On the one hand, Sure Start has been transformed from an early intervention policy to the provision of universal preschool services that integrate health, education, advice and support in Sure Start children's centres. From 2010 they will operate in 'every community', with a clear emphasis on social inclusion through work and a role to provide childcare for working parents. Underlying this approach is a differentiation of social exclusion into a number of subcategories: wide, deep and concentrated. The concept of wide social exclusion covers all those who suffer one of a range of disadvantages. The numbers who are socially excluded in this way are large, but New Labour is optimistic that its policies of social inclusion through paid work and welfare reform are successfully addressing this aspect of social exclusion. Sure Start children's centres are a part of this approach.

Those who suffer multiple forms of disadvantage, the deeply socially excluded, have more recently become a new focus for intervention policies. Their characterisation as having been left behind by a rising tide of material prosperity constructs their problems as having their origins in something other than poverty, and as not being susceptible to the solutions that are successfully addressing wide social exclusion. Whereas progress in relation to wide social exclusion is measured in terms of the numbers of *individuals* who have no Level 2 qualifications, who live in workless households or who are not in education, employment or training, the deeply excluded are counted in terms of the numbers of families. Policies have been introduced to identify these families and target them with new interventions. Here a moral underclass discourse of social exclusion is apparent, in which it is the social and cultural characteristics of families that are the subject of intervention and transformation. In this process, the policy emphasis on participation, empowerment and local control has been lost. Instead, the deeply excluded are increasingly the object of programmes devised by psychologists and tested using RCTs, thereby excluding (by controlling for) the effects of context (whether this is social, cultural or material) and focusing on changing the individual/family.

Coinciding with New Labour's refinement of the concept of social exclusion and the switch in policy approach were the disappointing findings of the first evaluation of Sure Start. The finding that the least disadvantaged families had benefited, even if only very moderately, from living in a Sure Start area, while the most disadvantaged had actually suffered additional disadvantage relative to their counterparts living outside a Sure Start area, contributed a justification for differentiating between different degrees of social exclusion and adopting different policy approaches for different groups. Replacing Sure Start as an early intervention policy for families with very young children is the more highly individually targeted FNP programme.

The findings of the second outcome evaluation of Sure Start, published in March 2008, came after a shift in policy in response, at least in part, to the findings of the first outcome study. The second evaluation found modest advantages for children living in Sure Start areas, which extended to all families in the area, not just the least disadvantaged. No adverse effects of the kind found in the first evaluation study were found in the later study. The authors argue that this may be because projects had had time to get established and known and trusted by families. The impatience of policy makers to find evidence of policy effectiveness to justify expenditure decisions means that policy has moved on before there has been time to really establish what works in terms of early intervention. The dominant discourse around social exclusion is increasingly that of the moral underclass, focused on drawing in the hard to reach and transforming them.

The original conception of Sure Start was one which, by targeting communities and areas rather than families or individuals, contained within it the possibility of addressing the broader social and material processes involved in social exclusion. These aspects of social exclusion were never made the subjects of the targets against which the success of Sure Start was to be measured and they are not aspects of Sure Start that feature in the national evaluation reports. Both the targets and the evaluation have concentrated on the transformation of maternal attitudes and behaviour as the means for preventing the reproduction of social exclusion. Nonetheless, the openness of the SSLPs to local control and direction made it possible to address processes beyond mothering that play an important role in social exclusion. The move to a universalised employment focus for early years provision, on the one hand, and a targeted 'problem family' approach, on the other, risks losing all acknowledgement of the continuing role of inequality in perpetuating social exclusion.

References

Belsky, J. and Melhuish, E. (2007) 'The impact of Sure Start Local Programmes on children and their families', in J. Belsky, J. Barnes and E. Melhuish (eds) *The national evaluation of Sure Start. Does area-based early intervention work?*, Bristol: The Policy Press.

Blair, T. (2006) 'Our sovereign value: fairness', Speech to the Joseph Rowntree Foundation, 5 September, www.number-10.gov.uk/output/Page10037.asp

Churchill, H. (2007) 'Children's services in 2006', in K. Clarke, T. Maltby and P. Kennett (eds) *Social Policy Review 19*, Bristol: The Policy Press.

Clarke, K. (2006) 'Childhood, parenting and early intervention: a critical examination of the Sure Start national programme', *Critical Social Policy*, vol 26, no 4, pp 699-721.

Clarke, K. (2007) 'From "cycles of disadvantage" to Sure Start: discourses of early intervention in families', *Critical Policy Analysis*, vol 1, no 2, pp 154-69.

DCSF (Department for Children Schools and Families) (2008) *Family Nurse Partnership 2008-09, recruitment of second wave of sites: Bidding process and criteria*, London: DCSF, www.everychildmatters.gov.uk/parents/healthledsupport

Glass, N. (1999) 'Sure Start: the development of an early intervention programme for young children in the United Kingdom', *Children and Society*, vol 13, pp 257-64.

Glass, N. (2005) 'Surely some mistake?', *The Guardian*, 5 January, www.guardian.co.uk/society/2005/jan/05/guardiansocietysupplement.childrensservices

HM Treasury (2003) *Every child matters*, Cm 5860, London: The Stationery Office.

HM Treasury (2004) *Choice for parents: The best start for children: A ten year strategy for childcare*, London: The Stationery Office.

Levitas, R. (2005) *The inclusive society? Social exclusion and New Labour* (2nd edition), Basingstoke: Palgrave Macmillan.

Levitas, R., Pantazis, C., Fahmy, E., Gordon, D., Lloyd, E. and Patsios, D. (2007) *The multi-dimensional analysis of social exclusion*, Report prepared for the Social Exclusion Unit, Bristol: University of Bristol, www.cabinetoffice.gov.uk/social_exclusion_task_force/publications/multidimensional.aspx.

Melhuish, E. and Hall, D. (2007) 'The policy background to Sure Start', in J. Belsky, J. Barnes and E. Melhuish (eds) *The national evaluation of Sure Start: Does area-based early intervention work?*, Bristol: The Policy Press.

Miliband, D. (2006) *Social exclusion: the next steps forward*, London: ODPM.

NESS (National Evaluation of Sure Start) (2005) *Early impacts of Sure Start Local Programmes on children and families: Report of the cross-sectional study on 9 and 36 month children and their families*, Sure Start Report no 13, London: DfES.

NESS (2008) *The impact of Sure Start Local Programmes on three year olds and their families*, Sure Start Report no 27, London: DFCS.

Parton, N. (2006) *Safeguarding childhood: Early intervention and surveillance in a late modern society*, Basingstoke: Palgrave Macmillan.

Pugh, G. (1998) 'Children at risk of becoming socially excluded: an introduction to the "problem"', *Comprehensive Spending Review: Cross-departmental review of provision for young children: Supporting papers (vol 1)*, London: HM Treasury.

Rutter, M. (2007) 'Sure Start Local Programmes: an outsider's perspective', in J. Belsky, J. Barnes and E. Melhuish (eds) *The national evaluation of Sure Start: Does area-based early intervention work?*, Bristol: The Policy Press.

Social Exclusion Task Force (2006) *Reaching out: An action plan on social exclusion*, London: Cabinet Office.

Social Exclusion Task Force (2007a) *Reaching out: Think family*, London: Cabinet Office.

Social Exclusion Task Force (2007b) *Reaching out: Progress on social exclusion*, London: Cabinet Office.

Social Exclusion Task Force (2008) *Think family: Improving the life chances of families at risk*, London: Cabinet Office.

Sure Start (2002) *Sure Start: A guide for sixth wave programmes*, London: DfES.

Ward, L. (2005) 'Doubts over value of £3bn Sure Start', *The Guardian*, 13 September.

Welshman, J. (2007) *From transmitted deprivation to social exclusion: Policy, poverty and parenting*, Bristol: The Policy Press.

Attachment research and the origins of violence: a story of damaged brains and damaged minds

Felicity de Zulueta

'The relevance lies not in the weapon they carry; it is in the mind that holds the weapon.' (anonymous)

There is little doubt that we belong to a species that has made the most amazing technological advances over the last few centuries: we can fly to the moon, we can communicate instantly across the globe, we can map our genome, and advances in medicine and sanitation mean that many of us live longer and healthier lives than our ancestors. And yet, despite such extraordinary skills and scientific advances, when it comes to understanding human behaviour, and especially violent behaviour, we seem to be groping in the dark.

The UK government is currently faced with a spate of knife violence and killings in London and other cities, which are being highly publicised by the media. We are told that knife crime has existed for hundreds of years, but that it has now reached a critical mass and, as a result of the media coverage, it is in our face on a daily basis and, more important, in the face of the young people who feel threatened by it. The government wants to be seen to be doing something to make us feel safer and has produced a £100 million *Youth crime action plan* (YCAP) (HM Government, 2008). But, even before the plan was published, researchers in the field of child violence were providing evidence that contradicted the core assumptions of government policy.

What is perhaps most extraordinary to someone like myself, brought up among the so-called primitive tribes of Dayaks and hunter gatherers of Borneo, is that, in this so-called civilised culture, we can countenance the sight of a 10-year-old coldly stabbing another child without realising that this is totally abnormal behaviour. How can it be that children in our communities live in such terror that they feel they have to carry a knife to protect themselves? They tell us that their fear is such that the furthest thing on their minds is being stopped by the police. How can a young man kill another simply because he feels 'disrespected'? Why aren't we asking ourselves the obvious questions: What is wrong with these kids? What is going on in their minds? As one wise young person is quoted as saying: 'The relevance lies not in the weapon they carry; it is in the mind that holds the weapon'.

But do we want to understand what is going on in their minds when the standard response is to label these individuals 'evil' and to punish them by 'locking them up'. We want them out of sight. In effect, we want them out of our minds. And to help us achieve this aim, politicians, the police and the press clamour for still more prisons, and the 'moral perspective' ends up overriding any thoughtful enquiry and any preventive action based on scientific research. Indeed, Western scientists have been providing us with information about how the human brain develops and functions for almost a quarter of a century. One would assume that understanding why we behave the way we do would be of great interest to parents, teachers and those who govern us. However, we have been ignoring their findings, both in terms of how we bring up children and in terms of government policy. Why?

The reasons for the failure of our society to absorb and to integrate this particular body of scientific evidence is almost as interesting as the neurobiological findings we now have relating to the origins of the high levels of violence to self and other that we face in the UK. Both are the subjects of this chapter.

Violence begets violence

What is the social context into which British children are born today? Most commentators now state that youth crime is fairly static, but violent crime is increasing, indeed some figures are stark: 25% of homicide victims are young men, usually victims of other young men; murder rates due to stabbing for the under-16s has risen by 25% (Smith and Allen, 2004; Roe and Ashe, 2008).

According to NHS figures, an average of 58 youngsters a day in England are being admitted to hospital after being deliberately injured, a rise from 16,600 in 2003 to 21,859 in 2007 (Revill, 2008). These figures do not include young people taken to casualty and sent home, nor those who die as a result of the harm. Much of this abuse is not investigated. Infants aged under one are more at risk of being killed at the hands of another person than any age group of child under 18 in England and Wales (Coleman et al, 2007).

According to a UNICEF (2003) report on child maltreatment and deaths, at least two children under the age of 15 die of abuse or neglect every week in the UK. The report also finds that poverty and stress, along with drug and alcohol abuse, appear to be the factors most closely associated with child abuse and neglect. Eighty per cent of the abusers are the children's biological parents and most of the children injured are babies and toddlers who are particularly vulnerable to violence from their parents or carers. It is important to note that the human male is more vulnerable than his female counterpart, both physically and emotionally.

In the same homes, adults are also at risk: two women die every week in the UK as a result of violence by their partner or former partner, and in one study 21% of women attending their general practitioner in East London reported having been raped (Coid et al, 2003). An Islington study revealed that one in three women had been 'punched, slapped, kicked, head-butted, suffered an attempt at strangulation or was struck by a weapon' (McCarney, 1996, p 1). Two out of three men in the same study said that they would use violence against their partners in a 'conflict situation' such as 'not having dinner on time'. The effects on children of witnessing parental abuse are very damaging for children, as we will see later. Sexual abuse is also of growing concern and usually involves more than one type of abuse, particularly emotional neglect. Child sexual abuse involving contact is estimated at 16% for girls and 7% for boys and is usually carried out by close relatives (Cawson et al, 2000).

So the world our children are born into is one with very high levels of domestic violence compared to other wealthy European countries and the impact on children is very high. For example, according to figures in a report by the Camelot Foundation and the Mental Health Foundation (2006), there has been a rise in admissions for self-harming behaviour from 11,891 in 2002-03 to 15,955 in 2006-07, with three times as many admissions for girls as for boys aged 10 to 18 years; among 10-year-olds admitted for self-harm, boys outnumbered girls. The forms of self-harm recorded by hospitals are drugs overdose, attempted hanging and deliberate injury with a sharp object. Self-harming behaviour is often self-directed violence and it can be, as will be shown later, an attempt to relieve severe distress. Finally, current evidence in the UK shows that inequalities in health are widening as a result of current economic policies (www.dh.gov.uk/en/Publichealth/Healthinequalities/index.htm).

This is important because of the repeated finding that inequality as such is bad for the health of the nation whatever the absolute material standards. Rising suicide rates, increased levels of crime, drug misuse and violence, particularly homicide in young men, are the likely result (Watt, 1996).

Unfortunately, despite Tony Blair's stated aim in 1998 to end child poverty forever, a report by the London Child Poverty Commission (2008) states that almost a third of children in Britain and more than two out of five in London and half in inner London are still living below the official poverty line. These children are more likely to fail at school, end up without a job and get caught up in anti-social behaviour (ASB) and crime.

As if these figures were not enough to convince us of the need to take the causes of violence seriously, we now have some important evidence showing how violence impacts on the health of a nation. Feletti and his colleagues carried out a large series of prospective studies in the US looking at the relationship between adverse childhood experiences and adult health, well-being, social function and healthcare (Feletti and Anda, 2008). In these studies, adverse childhood experiences were found to be the following:

Abuse:	Emotional abuse
	Physical abuse
	Sexual abuse
Neglect:	Physical or emotional
Household dysfunction:	Mother treated violently
	Household use of drugs or alcohol
	Presence of mental illness
	Parental separation or divorce
	Incarcerated household member

The authors found that the more adverse childhood experiences an individual has endured, the more they are likely to suffer from severe obesity, ischaemic heart disease, stroke, chest diseases, diabetes, hepatitis, sexually transmitted diseases and depression. They are also more likely to smoke, abuse alcohol and drugs and attempt suicide. Similarly, the more adverse childhood experiences an individual has endured, the greater the risk of:

- being sexually assaulted as an adult (especially if a woman);
- being a victim of domestic violence (more so for women than men); and
- perpetrating domestic violence (for both men and women).

These figures speak for themselves, and studies on adverse childhood experiences should be on the reading list of every politician, assuming they have one. We can conclude that the less we protect our young from being neglected and abused, both physically and emotionally, the more they damage their lives through ill-health and the more they damage others through violent behaviour.

Feletti and Anda report that their team developed their research on adverse childhood events after finding that, in their weight-reducing programme, the high drop-out rate was limited exclusively to patients who were *successfully losing weight*. They wondered why. As a result of their studies, summarised in the report mentioned above, they recognised that certain of the most intractable public health problems like obesity were unconscious, or occasionally conscious, solutions dating back to the earliest years, but hidden by time, by shame, by secrecy and by social taboos against exploring certain areas of life experience. It became 'evident that traumatic life experiences during childhood and adolescence were far more common than generally recognised, were complexly interrelated, and were associated in a strong proportionate manner to outcomes important to medical practice, public health and the social fabric of the nation' (Feletti and Anda, 2008, pp 2-3).

The mind of a 'thug'

If we are to begin to make sense of the behaviour of some of the children who kill one another, we need to know who they are. This is, in great part, determined by what they have been through, and this is the story the media never give you.

Emma was 15 when she was caught as part of a gang involved in kicking a young man to death. Who was Emma? Imagine a child born to a teenage mother living on an estate where drugs and violence were the norm. The mother is on drugs or drinks in order to cope with her nightmares and her daily intrusive memories of being beaten up and raped by Emma's father and his mates. Emma was also beaten and saw what her father did to her mother. Her mother could not protect her and blamed her for being 'such a waste of time'. Emma was bright, but sitting in class proved to be a waste of time because she could not make sense of what the teacher said. She could hardly focus on the work and she could not remember anything anyway. Also, in the breaks, there were always boys making nasty rude comments about her, and the girls bullied and mocked her incessantly. She tried to tell a teacher what she was going through but the teacher told her to just try and be strong and forget it. She stopped going to school: 'What was the point,' she said, 'I just felt stupid'.

When Emma was 12, her mother went to live with another man and he did not want Emma around. Her grandmother, who had been kind to her, had died. Her father or his friends were looking for her to rape her. She took to living more and more on the streets and found herself with other children like her, and they looked after each other, in their sort of way, stealing food and alcohol to fight off the flashbacks of their frightening past. The problem was that Emma got involved in carrying drugs to get some money and, because her nightmares were so bad and her mind was so 'hyped up', she started to take them too and then had to give herself to the dealers to pay for the drugs. At times, she felt so desperate she would cut herself and then she felt a momentary peace. But it did not last long. She moved from one group of children to another, in search of safety and company, but it was scary because the bigger boys wanted sex from her and then there were the fights. The gang leaders made it clear you were either with them or you could be treated as outsiders were treated. Several times she saw boys she knew being attacked with knives and once she was threatened by a guy who thought she was laughing at him.

Emma became more and more terrified, hyper-alert, looking for danger everywhere she went. It would just take a look or a gesture and a fight would start. Everyone was on edge, trying to survive and at times fighting for their lives. You could trust no one, certainly not the adults. The police never helped; they just took your knife away or took you to the prison and locked you in a cell. That was hell because, with nothing to do, the flashbacks and nightmares got so bad that Emma began to believe all the horrible things she was seeing were really happening and she heard the voices of her father and his mates laughing at her and threatening her. She was desperate to get out of the cell and to get back onto the drugs; they were the only things that worked for her and kept the nightmares away.

Emma's behaviour illustrates what happens to traumatised minds and how some children cope with the symptoms. As Teicher (2000, p 67) said: 'Our brains are sculpted by our early experiences. Maltreatment is a chisel that shapes the brain to contend with strife but at the cost of enduring wounds'. The human brain does not develop in a vacuum: it responds and interacts with its environment as it grows in the womb and then within the context of a family and a community. It has specific needs if it is to grow to its full potential. If those needs are not fulfilled and if the brain is further damaged by what it is subjected to during the developmental process, the result will be the production of a dysfunctional brain: violent behaviour is only one of such a brain's many manifestations.

The effects of maltreatment on brain development

As soon as they are born, human infants, like other mammals, are genetically predisposed to want access or proximity to an attachment figure, especially when they are frightened or in need. When reunited with their caregivers or, later, with those they love, they have a nice reassuring warm feeling largely produced by endogenous opiates. Separation leads to distress and a decrease in those endogenous opiates. Panksepp et al (1985, p 25) described social bonding as an 'opiate addiction'.

Caregiver–infant attunement within a secure attachment

Research on attachment is based on many studies of both primate and human behaviour, the earliest of which were Harlow's 'mother–infant separation experiments' on rhesus monkeys (Harlow, 1974). The earlier and the longer the infants were separated from their mother, the worse the long-term effects on their behaviour. These infants showed self-destructive and self-stimulating behaviour (that is, rocking and head-banging movements), a failure to discriminate social cues and grossly abnormal and ASB in adulthood. If artificially inseminated, the female monkeys were observed mutilating or even killing their infants. These findings were used by Bowlby (1988) to develop his view that attachment behaviour is fundamental to our understanding of human behaviour. His theory has now been backed up by over 20 years of research in the field.

The brain substrate of attachment behaviour essentially involves a large part of the right hemisphere and, in particular, the supraorbital area of the brain, which is crucial to our capacity to empathise with others, and the limbic system and paralimbic system. The infant brain is moulded by its earliest experiences with its caregiver(s). It is the caregiver's capacity to attune to the infant's signals that is so crucial in the first two years of life. This is achieved by holding, caressing, smiling, stimulating or calming the infant. The stimulation and affect modulation that takes place between caregiver and infant is what enables the infant brain to develop the capacity both to modulate affect and to identify and communicate emotional states.

The caregiver also demonstrates reflective functioning by giving meaning to the infant's experiences and predicting their behaviour. This interaction results in a child who can put himself (or herself) in the mind of another. It enables people to understand each other in terms of their mental states, to interact successfully and to develop a sense of agency and continuity (Fonagy and Target, 1997). These infants are securely attached and this will protect them from developing post-traumatic stress disorder (PTSD) in potentially traumatic situations (Schore, 1996, 2001; Siegel, 2001). Fonagy and Target (1997) also provide evidence that, even if a child has a deprived or abusive family life, the empathic understanding coming from an outsider (teacher, health worker or relative) can compensate for the effects of childhood abuse and protect against future re-enactment and future traumatisation.

The 'sculpting' of the infant brain that takes place during the first two years of an infant's life is one during which its 50 trillion brain synapses present at birth explode into a 1,000 trillion synapses, a huge increase in brain connections resulting from the combined interaction of both genetically induced developmental pathways and the external stimulation and emotional modulation provided by the infant's attachment figures. Some of the synapses are formed and 'hardwired' as a result of stimulation, while others are 'pruned' or dissolved due to the lack of it. The effects of severe emotional neglect and absence of stimulation were starkly illustrated by the brain scans of Romanian orphans, which showed black empty spaces in the supraorbital areas.

The laying down of future templates of attachment behaviour

The daily interactions between infant and caregiver provide the memories that the infant's brain synthesises into what Bowlby (1988) called 'working models'. These are internal representations or templates of how the attachment figure, and subsequent attachment figures, will be expected to respond to the child's attachment behaviour. They were identified through the work of Ainsworth et al (1978) and Main and Hesse

(1992) observing the response of one-year-old infants when separated and then reunited with their caregivers in the 'Strange Situation'.[1]

Sroufe and his colleagues concluded from their study on four year olds that these 'working models' are internalised whole relationships (Troy and Sroufe, 1987). This means that insecurely attached individuals can recreate their attachment experience either from the perspective of the victim or from the perspective of the abuser, depending on the context they are in. An important finding in their study is that the secure children did not become either bullies or victims, unlike their insecure counterparts: bullying or being bullied appears to be the prerogative of the insecurely attached.

Wounds of the mind in children who have been abused

Parents vary in how they bring up their children, and their infants develop different strategies to gain proximity to their caregivers in order to survive. These are: the anxious ambivalent response; the avoidant response; and the disorganised response (Ainsworth et al, 1978; Main and Hesse, 1992). We will focus on the last two attachment patterns as potential sources of violence. Essentially, the less the caregiver has their child's mind in their mind, the more damage they can inflict to the developing brain of their infant.

The avoidant attachment

Twenty to twenty-five per cent of Ainsworth et al's (1978) middle-class sample experienced rejection when in need of their parent. By the age of one they had developed an apparent indifference to being separated from their attachment figure in the Strange Situation. However, their elevated heart rate betrayed their separation anxiety. Most of these children developed conduct disorders and tended to deny the importance of attachment relations. They also tended to be bullies (Sroufe, 2005).

Children sent to boarding school at an early age can develop this form of attachment behaviour in order to cope with the premature separation from their parents and families: the resulting 'stiff upper lip' attitude to life was invaluable in the making of officers in the days of the Empire. However, their limited experience of normal family and community life may contribute to the difficulty politicians and civil servants have in understanding, let alone tackling, the problems of violence in the community.

The disorganised attachment: psychological trauma in childhood

Around 15% of Main and Hesse's (1992) sample of infants showed a 'disorganised' response in relation to their caregiver's return following separation in the Strange

Situation: they often froze in trance-like states like adults suffering from PTSD. Their caregivers were frightening either because they directly abused their child or because they themselves suffered from the effects of psychological trauma or PTSD.

A mother's nightmare revisited

A Turkish mother, who was suffering from symptoms of PTSD following being raped in prison, reported how her child, a product of the rape, would remind her at times of the rapist. At such times she would find herself reliving the horror of her past, unable to care for or comfort her infant who was subjected to her terrified and angry emotions.

This type of parental behaviour leaves the child in a state of fear without solution in that both the attachment response and the fear response are activated simultaneously (Main and Hesse, 1992).

What do we mean by this?

The origin of dissociation

In the face of a terrifying parent who is abusing them emotionally or physically, the child, like any mammal, has three options: to fight, to flee or to freeze, all responses dictated by the autonomic system of our reptilian brain with little or no involvement of the cortex or thinking brain.

As Perry et al (1995) describe, the infant psychobiological response to feeling threatened by their caregiver involves three stages:

(1) The fight–flight response mediated by the sympathetic system. This bypasses the cortical centres and their capacity for symbolic processing with the result that traumatic experiences are stored in somatic, behavioural and affective systems. These expereiences will be relived later in the form of somatic flashbacks.

(2) If the fight–flight response is not possible, as will usually be the case with a small vulnerable child, the parasympathetic state takes over and the child 'freezes', which, in nature, may be linked to feigning death in order to survive. Vocalisation tends also to be inhibited and children, like young animals, may lose the capacity to speak and become mute, a phenomenon that is related to the release of endogenous opiates and the shutting down of the speech area, as observed in the positron emission tomography (PET) scans on adult patients suffering from PTSD (Rauch et al, 1996).

(3) Finally, when attacked or rejected by their caregiver, the infant is in a state of 'fear without solution' where both the above responses are activated, leading to a dissociative response (Main and Hesse, 1992). By this I mean that children, in fear of their caregiver's hatred and violence, can only maintain their vital attachment

to this desperately needed caregiver by resorting to 'dissociation', that is, creating different representations of themselves in relation to their caregiver. This results in a lack of self-continuity in relation to the 'other', as can be seen in patients suffering from a borderline personality disorder (Fonagy and Target, 1997; Ogawa et al, 1997; Ryle, 1997; Zulueta, 1999), complex PTSD (Herman, 1992a, 1992b) or developmental trauma (Van der Kolk, 2005). In other words, in order to ensure their survival, these terrified infants will develop an idealised (and often unconscious) attachment to their caregiver, on whom they continue to rely on in their minds, while all their terrifying 'self–other interactions' with the same caregiver become dissociated or unavailable to the conscious self. The result is a fragmented self.

The dissociated experiences will be relived in the form of flashbacks or nightmares when triggered into conscience by a memory or some sensory reminder, such as going to bed at night for the child who has been sexually abused, or being humiliated or made to feel helpless.

People with childhood PTSD will also re-traumatise themselves in some desperate attempt to gain control or as a means to get a chemical fix through the release of endogenous opiates; this is also the case for adults with PTSD. This is because, in certain life-threatening situations, our bodies can release endogenous opiates to produce analgesia. This also happens when traumatised individuals re-traumatise themselves through either cutting themselves or by using other forms of self-injury or traumatic re-enactments in order to get a 'high' and thereby cope with the unbearable feelings they cannot modulate (Van der Kolk, 1996).

The 'moral defence'

At a cognitive level, these children, and later adults, will tend to blame themselves and feel guilty rather than blame their caregiver for what happened to them. By taking the blame and being 'bad', and thereby keeping the caregiver as an idealised figure in their mind, these children gain a sense of control in the face of unbearable helplessness. They also preserve the hope that in the future, if they behave well, they will finally get the love and care they did not have. This cognitive defence, aptly called the 'moral defence' by Fairbairn (1952), is ferociously maintained in order to avoid the unbearable realisation that there is really no such idealised parent, a discovery that leads to grief and a sense of hopelessness.

The traumatic attachment

The cost to both child and adult of maintaining this 'traumatic attachment' to the abusing or neglectful parent is a heavy one. In seeking the parental care they never had, these individuals will tend to destroy available intimate adult relationships. They will also tend to sabotage their achievements, and any progress they may make in treatment, in order to continue their search for the idealised parent they still yearn for, albeit unconsciously (Zulueta, 2006a). This is why the successful weight-losers dropped out of the programme in the study on adverse childhood experiences mentioned above (Feletti and Anda, 2008). In some cases, this inner conflict and resulting sense of intense vulnerability can also lead, paradoxically, to homicide (Zulueta, 2006a, 2006b, pp 137-51). Addressing this 'traumatic attachment' and its cognitive distortions may well be central to the treatment of patients with a history of child abuse or severe neglect.

Traumatic attachment: triggering violent behaviour in an adult

Dr X had done some therapeutic work with A, a 43-year-old single man who was imprisoned for killing his friend while out stealing in the countryside. On being interviewed by Dr X, A gave a history of being 'battered' by his mother when a child. He had admitted that he was frightened of her and had begun to make links between his fear and his violent behaviour.

The therapist then said, 'Say your mother was sitting over there, what would you say to her?' The patient developed a marked fear response, very similar to that of a small child, and he said that he was unable to imagine himself saying to an imaginary mother in the room: 'Mother, you can't hit me any more. I am an adult'. 'What would stop you?' asks the therapist. 'Fear,' replies the big man in front of him. 'Fear of what? What is she going to do?', asks his therapist. 'Well she might get up and clout me.'

Even after admitting that his mother is now an 85-year-old fragile little woman compared to him, he says that he cannot disagree with her, let alone hit her. A is speaking and behaving like a small boy and, although he does seem aware of the fact that his fear of his old mother is irrational, the reality is that, at that moment in time, faced with his imaginary mother, the mother in his head, he can only admit to fear, the fear of a child who is terrified of being battered.

As it turns out, this man battered his friend to death when the latter insisted that they spend the night in the comfort of his mother's house and 'mouthed' Lenny when he refused (Zulueta, 2006a).

Lost for words

Henry (1997) has noted that many patients suffering from developmental PTSD also suffered from alexithymia, which is defined as an inability to describe emotions in words and symbols in order to cope with disturbing feelings. As a result, such patients will show a tendency to re-enact their traumatic experience rather than think. The resulting effect is that of re-traumatisation (Van der Kolk, 1996). Alexithymia appears to be associated with an inter-hemispheric transfer deficit (Zeitlin et al, 1989) and is more likely to occur if the trauma is repeated, as in sexual abuse (Zeitlin et al, 1993).

Inability to regulate emotions

The loss or inability to regulate intense feelings is probably the most far-reaching effect of a failure of attunement in infancy following repeated traumatisation (Van der Kolk, 1996, 2005). As a result, these children have little capacity to modulate sympathetic dominant affects like terror, rage and even elation, or parasympathetic dominant affects like shame, disgust and despair.

Shame, when it is the emotional reaction to a self that has been totally invalidated, is extremely important in triggering violent reactions in victims of chronic neglect and abuse. The basic cause of violent behaviour is the wish to ward off or eliminate the feelings of shame or humiliation – feelings that are painful and that can even be intolerable and overwhelming – and replace them with the opposite – feelings of power and pride. 'I was disrespected,' said a murderer. 'Better be bad than not at all' (Gilligan, 1996, p 29).

Persistent fear response and hyper-arousal

The result of early and repeated traumatisation of a child's brain produces changes in the neurochemical systems of the brain that lead to poor attention and concentration, disturbed sleep and poor impulse control and fine motor control. This chronic activation of the brain can lead to a reduction in size of the hippocampus, which is involved in cognition and memory (Perry, 2000).

The combined effect of repeated re-traumatisation and the reliving of the traumatic experiences in the form of flashbacks and nightmares sets the brain into a state of quasi-permanent hyper-arousal. The child's brain has become adapted to a world that is unpredictable and dangerous; it is hyper-vigilant, focused on non-verbal cues that may be threatening (Perry et al, 1995), particularly cues that are linked to earlier traumatic experiences. In this way, a 'look', a gesture, may be enough to trigger the child into a state of re-enactment in which he (and his knife) do to the other what was once done to them. The act of murder in a state of dissociation bypasses the thinking brain as the child gains control over his terror: the 'other' lying in a pool of blood on the sidewalk is not the human being that you and I see: he is the threat of the past that has to be eliminated.

The regions of the brain involved in hyper-arousal are always 'on', and because of this the child may frequently experience hyperactivity, anxiety, impulsivity and sleep problems (Perry et al, 1995). To learn and incorporate new information, whether it be a lesson or a new social experience, the brain must be in a state of 'attentive calm', a state a traumatised child rarely achieves. For this reason, many of these otherwise intelligent children are diagnosed with learning disabilities (Perry, 1999).

Males are more likely to display 'fight and flight' responses and tachycardia when exposed to fearful experiences (Perry et al, 1995). But, in some adolescent boys, the damage is so profound that their heart rate normalises over time and some report a 'soothing' feeling when they begin 'stalking' a potential victim (Perry et al, 1997). This reaction was reported following the murder of a Londoner by two adolescents, when one of them said that he got a 'buzz' when stalking his victim. It may also relate to a study on criminal men, which showed lower heart rates than controls or anti-social men (Raine et al, 1995).

Females are more likely to dissociate when exposed to a traumatic event and internalise their symptoms, that is, present with depression and self-destructive behaviour (Perry et al, 1995). However, as they grow older, they too can become hyper-aroused.

Visible brain damage

The brains of severely deprived and abused children are significantly smaller than those of non-abused children. The limbic system (which governs emotions) can be 20% to 30% smaller and tends to have fewer synapses. Similarly, the hippocampus (responsible for memory) is smaller in many abused children. There is also increased activity in the locus coeruleus (responsible for hair-trigger alert) in children from violent families (Shaw and Winslow, 1997).

Prevention based on a model of violence as a disease

Transmission through the cycle of violence

The longer we avoid tackling the origins of violence in our society, the worse the outcome. Violence can be best understood as a disease, as a symptom of a dysfunctional society (Zulueta, 1998). As we saw in the studies on adverse childhood experiences, the consequences of violence are many and costly, both to the individual sufferer and to society. The worst aspect is that the 'virus' of violence can be transmitted down the generations through the attachment system. Van Ijzendoorn and Bakermans-Kranenberg (1997) showed that there is a 75% correspondence between parents' mental representations of attachment (using the Adult Attachment Interview developed by Main and Hesse, 1992) and their infants' attachment security. Mothers suffering from PTSD due to childhood abuse or adult traumas transmit their low levels of cortisol to their offspring, predisposing them to developing PTSD in later life (Yehuda, 1997; Yehuda et al, 2002, 2005).

Manifestations of the disease

Children who have been abused or neglected are considerably more likely to have personality disorders and high symptom levels in early adulthood (Weiler and Widom, 1996; Johnson et al, 1999). Sroufe's 19-year prospective study on disorganised infants shows that they tend to develop dissociative disorders such as borderline personality disorders or other dissociative disorders (Ogawa et al, 1997). People with childhood histories of trauma make up almost the entire criminal justice population in the US (Teplin et al, 2002). I believe that figures for the UK are not very different. Three quarters of the perpetrators of child sexual abuse have been sexually abused in childhood (Romano and De Luca, 1997).

Who is at risk and when to intervene?

The seeds of violence are laid down in the first two years of life. It is important to remember that male infants are physically and emotionally more vulnerable than their female counterparts and that male aggressive behaviour is highly stable as early as the age of two.

In hospital, if a baby shows neurological signs of impairment and has a mother who is depressed, domestically abused, a single teenager, on drugs or alcohol or all of these things, the mother is considered to be a risk to her baby. In the Dunedin study (Moffit and Caspi, 1998), trained nurses observing three-year-old children at play for 90 minutes were able to identify those 'at risk': they were restless and negative, and lacked persistence and attention. At age 21, males in the 'at-risk' group were compared with other 21-year-olds: 47% abused their partners (compared with 9.5% of others); three times as many had an anti-social personality; two and a half times as many had two or more criminal convictions. Fifty-five per cent of offences committed by the 'at-risk' group were violent compared with 18% of others. The 'at-risk' group not only committed many more violent offences, but also much more severe ones, such as robbery, rape and homicide (Moffit and Caspi, 1998).

Fewer of the females became conduct-disordered, but, where they did, 30% of the 'at-risk' group had teenage births (the others had none) and 43% were in violent, abusive relationships (Caspi et al, 1996). The authors conclude that immature mothers with no strong parenting skills, and violent partners, have already borne the next generation of 'at risk' children (Caspi et al, 1996).

In a study by Shaw and Winslow (1997), low maternal responsiveness, that is, low attunement, predicted the following in the infant:

   at 1.5 years: aggression, non-compliance, tantrums
   at 2 years: lower compliance, attention getting, hitting
   at 3 years: problems with other children

at 3.5 years: higher coercive behaviour

at 6 years: fighting and stealing.

We now know that the earlier the interventions in helping parents to attune with their infants (that is, during pregnancy and infancy), the less expensive and the more effective they are. Many of these interventions are reviewed by the Wave Trust (www.wavetrust.org) and many American websites, but a recent short intervention in the Netherlands stands out for being effective, cheap and user-friendly. It is a sensitivity-focused intervention of up to only 16 sessions and no more, which succeeds in reducing disorganised attachment and promoting secure attachment in infants. The Dutch team achieve this by introducing a trained worker to the family – who could be a health visitor, for instance – and by using a video-feedback intervention to promote positive parenting (VIPP), focusing on those moments when the mother attunes to her child. The model has been extended to ways of sensitively disciplining infants and toddlers. The reason why the method is effective and popular is that the parent is her own model and her sensitive behaviour is reinforced so that she feels she is doing the right thing (Bakerman-Kranenburg et al, 2008). The parent is not made to feel that they are bad or criminal, unlike many targeted parents in the UK.

By the time children are going to school and are in the community, what do we look for in terms of risk for future violent behaviour? Children who are neglected physically and psychologically, left alone without adequate supervision and whose parents are involved in drugs, the justice system or who are mentally ill are at risk. Once at school, we look for those kids who do not do well, who truant, bully, are involved in alcohol, drugs and gangs and who are arrested for delinquency. But, by this point, intervention is more difficult and costly. So we lock them up and make them worse. However, what youths in South London asked for, according to a recent Dispatches survey, was more job opportunities, more and better youth clubs and sports facilities, better control and discipline from parents, more police on the streets and more help for gang members to leave their violent lifestyle (Channel 4 News, 2008).

Conclusions

Empathy is key to understanding violence. By their first year, infants can react to suffering by showing empathy, indifference or hostility. Violent offenders show little or no empathy at all because they do not experience themselves or 'others' as human beings. This is the nub of the problem and one that people find hard to accept.

Since violence is triggered in high-propensity people by social factors (poverty, drugs, alcohol, television) that are difficult to change, reducing the number of people with a propensity to violence would make strategic sense. If violence costs the UK more than £20 billion per annum (Lord Bassam, 2001) and the cost of locking up a child with severe 'conduct disorder' is around £100,000 per annum, one would imagine that there would be a purely financial incentive in going for prevention in the UK.

And yet the ratio of the current cost of preventing of crime compared to the cost of its consequences is 1:300. If we are to take these figures seriously, it is clear that violence is here to stay: in the UK the well-being of our children is apparently of little concern.

Compared to other European countries, the UK has a very low age of criminal responsibility and high numbers of children are locked up. Most professionals working in the area of criminal justice agree that too many children are being criminalised and brought into the youth justice system too early. As other contributors to this volume assert, the UK needs to adopt a strategy that reduces the custody of young people and uses the vast resources spent on prisons for preventive work in the community.

The fact that these unhappy children become the criminals, patients, parents and voters of the future does not mean that anything will change because, as I have pointed out, the more neglected or abused we may have been, the less likely we are to acknowledge it and the more likely we are to cling to the belief that our parents were right, that what we need is more punishment. Since many British politicians and civil servants have been brought up in private boarding schools, cut off from their families and from the rough and tumble of British multi-ethnic city life, with very little real experience of inner-city life, they are likely to follow the same inclination as their ancestors in the pursuit of law and order and aim 'to clamp down on knife crime' and 'curb street gangs' and build still more prisons, following closely our American model.

There is, however, one small hope. By being exposed to some of the terror our deprived children feel and express through their callous actions, a sufficient number of leaders with a vision of a better future for us all may turn to the scientific evidence at hand and invest in long-term prevention.

Note

[1] The 'Strange Situation' test: a mother and child are put in a room together full of toys under observation (Episode 1 and 2). A stranger is then introduced to see how the infant responds (Episode 3). The mother then leaves the room unobtrusively so that her infant is alone with the stranger (Episode 4). How does the infant respond to the mother's first departure? Mother returns, greeting and comforting the infant, encouraging her to play again. Mother leaves the room again, saying 'bye, bye' (Episode 5). The infant is alone for the second separation episode (Episode 6). The stranger returns (Episode 7) and then the mother and infant are reunited (Episode 8) (Ainsworth et al, 1978).

References

Ainsworth, M.D.S., Blehar, M.C., Waters, E. and Wall, S. (1978) *Patterns of attachment: A psychological study of the Strange Situation*, Hillsdale, NJ: Lawrence Erlbaum Associates.

Bakerman-Kranenburg, M.J., Van Ijzendoorn, M.H. and Juffer, F. (2008) *Promoting positive parenting*, Abingdon: Taylor & Francis.

Bowlby, J. (1988) *A secure base: Clinical applications of attachment theory*, London: Routledge.

Camelot Foundation and the Mental Health Foundation (2006) *Truth hurts: Report of the national inquiry into self-harm in young people*, London: Camelot Foundation and the Mental Health Foundation.

Caspi, A., Moffitt, T.E., Newman, D.L. and Silva, P.A. (1996) 'Behavioural observations at age 3 years predict adult psychiatric disorders', *Archives of General Psychiatry*, vol 53, pp 1033-9.

Cawson, P., Watta, C., Brooker, S. and Kelly, G. (2000) *Child maltreatment in the United Kingdom: A study of the prevalence of child abuse and neglect*, London: NSPCC.

Channel 4 News (2008) *Dispatches survey into youth on youth serious violence: 100 youths in south London*, 28 January, www.channel4.com/news/media/current_affairs/pdfs/whykidskill20surveyresults.pdf

Coleman, K., Jansson, K., Kaiza, P. and Reed, E. (2007) *Homicides, firearms offences and intimate violence 2005/2006: Supplementary volume 1 to Crime in England and Wales 2005/2006*, London: Home Office.

Coid, J., Petruckevitch, A., Chung, W.-S., Richardson, J. Moorey, S., Cotter. S. and Feder, G.S. (2003) 'Sexual violence against adult women primary care attendants in east London', *British Journal of General Practice*, vol 53, pp 858-62.

Department of Health: Health Inequalities website (www.dh.gov.uk/en/Publichealth/Healthinequalities/index.htm).

Fairbairn, R. (1952) *Psychoanalytic study of the personality*, London: Routledge & Kegan Paul.

Feletti, P. and Anda, R. (2008) 'The relationship of adverse childhood experiences to adult health, well being, social function and healthcare', in Lanius/Vermetten (eds) *The hidden epidemic: The impact of early life trauma on health and disease*, Cambridge: Cambridge University Press.

Fonagy, P. and Target, M. (1997) 'Attachment and reflective function: their role in self organisation', *Development and Psychopathology*, vol 9, no 4, pp 679-700.

Gilligan, J. (1996) *Violence, our deadly epidemic and its causes*, New York: G.P. Putnam's Sons.

Harlow, H.F. (1974) *Learning to love* (2nd edn), New York/London: Jason Aronson.

Henry, J. (1997) 'Psychological and physiological responses to stress: the right hemisphere and the hypothalamic-pituitary-adrenal-axis, an inquiry into problems of human bonding', *Acta Physiologica Scandinavica*, vol 161, pp 164-9.

Herman, J.L. (1992a) 'Complex PTSD: a syndrome in survivors of prolonged and repeated trauma', *Journal of Traumatic Stress*, vol 5, pp 377-91.

Herman, J.L. (1992b) *Trauma and recovery: The aftermath of violence from domestic abuse to political terror*, New York: Basic Books.

HM Government (2008) *Youth crime action plan 2008*, London: COI.

Johnson, J.G., Cohen, P., Brown, J., Smailes, E.M. and Bernstein, D.P. (1999) 'Childhood maltreatment increases risk for personality disorders during early adulthood', *Archives of General Psychiatry*, vol 56, pp 600-6.

London Child Poverty Commission (2008) *Capital gains*, London: London Councils.

Lord Bassam (2001) House of Lords debate, 31 January.

Main, M. and Hesse, E. (1992) 'Disorganised/disorientated infant behaviour in the Strange Situation: lapses in monitoring of reasoning and discourse during the parent's adult attachment interview, and dissociative states', in M. Ammanati and D. Stern (eds) *Attachment and psychoanalysis*, Rome: Gius Laterza and Figli, pp 86-140.

McCarney, W. (1996) 'Domestic violence', *British Juvenile and Family Court Society Newsletter*, 1-3 April.

Moffitt, T.E. and Caspi, A. (1998) 'Annotation: implications of violence between intimate partners for child psychologists and psychiatrists', *Journal of Child Psychology and Psychiatry*, vol 39, no 2, pp 137-44.

Ogawa, J.R., Sroufe, L.A., Weinfield, N.S., Carlson, E.A. and Egeland, B. (1997) 'Development of the fragmented self: longitudinal study of dissociative symptomatology in a non clinical sample', *Development and Psychopathology*, vol 9, pp 855-79.

Panksepp, J., Siviy, S.M. and Normansell, L.A. (1985) 'Brain opioids and social emotions', in M. Reite and T. Field (eds) *The psychobiology of attachment and separation* (pp 3-49), London: Academic Press.

Perry, B.D. (1999) 'Memories of fear: how the brain stores and retrieves physiologic states, feelings, behaviors and thoughts from traumatic events', in J. Goodwin and R. Attia (eds) *Splintered reflections: Images of the body in trauma*, Boulder, CO: Basic Books.

Perry, B.D. (2001) 'The neurodevelopmental impact of violence in childhood', in D. Schetky and E. Benedek (eds) *Textbook of child and adolescent forensic psychiatry*, Washington, DC: American Psychiatric Press.

Perry, B.D., Arvinte, A., Marcellus, J. and Pollard, R.A. (1997) 'Syncope, bradycardia, cataplexiy and paralysis: sensitisation of an opioid – mediated dissociative response following childhood trauma', *Journal of the American Academy of Child and Adolescent Psychiatry*.

Perry, B.D., Pollard, R.A., Blakeley, T.L., Baker, W.L. and Vigilante, D. (1995) 'Childhood trauma, the neurobiology of adaptation, and 'use-dependent' development of the brain: how "states" become "traits"', *Infant Mental Health Journal*, vol 16, pp 271-91.

Povey, D. and colleagues (2001) *Recorded crime statistics: England and Wales, Home Office Statistical Bulletin 18/99*, London: Home Office (www.homeoffice.gov.uk/rds/pdfs/hosb1801.pdf).

Raine, A., Venables, P.H. and Williams, M. (1995) 'High autonomic arousal and electrodermal orienting at age 15 years as a protective factor against criminal behaviour at age 29 years', *American Journal of Psychiatry*, vol 152, pp 1595-1600.

Rauch, S.L., Van der Kolk, B.A., Fisler, R.E., Albert, N.M., Orr, S.P., Savage, C.R., Fischman, A.J., Jenike, M.A. and Pitman, R.K. (1996) 'A symptom provocation study of post traumatic stress disorder using positron emission tomography and script driven imagery', *Archives of General Psychiatry*, vol 53, pp 380-7.

Revill, J. (2008) 'Shock rise in violence against UK's children', *The Observer*, 20 July.

Roe, S. and Ashe, J. (2008) *Young people and crime: Findings from the 2006 Offending, Crime and Justice Survey*, Statistical Bulletin, London: Home Office.

Romano, E. and De Luca, R.V. (1997) 'Exploring the relationship between childhood sexual abuse and adult sexual perpetration', *Journal of Family Violence*, vol 12, pp 85-98.

Ryle, A. (1997) 'The structure and development of borderline personality disorder: a proposed model', *British Journal of Psychiatry*, vol 170, pp 82-7.

Schore, A.N. (1996) 'Experience dependent maturation of a regulatory system in the orbital pre-frontal cortex and the origin of developmental psychopathology', *Development and Psychopathology*, vol 8, pp 59-87.

Schore, A.N. (2001) 'The effects of early relational trauma on right brain development, affect regulation, and infant mental health', *Infant Mental Health Journal*, vol 22, pp 201-69.

Shaw, D.S. and Winslow, E.B. (1997) 'Precursors and correlates of antisocial behaviour from infancy to preschool', in D.M. Stoff, J. Breiling and J.D. Maser (eds) *Handbook of antisocial behaviour*, New York: Wiley.

Siegel, D.J. (2001) 'Toward an interpersonal neurobiology of the developing mind: attachment relationships, "mindsight", and neural integration', *Infant Mental Health Journal*, vol 22, pp 67-94.

Sroufe, A.L. (2005) 'Attachment and development: a prospective longitudinal study from birth to adulthood', *Attachment and Human Development*, vol 7, pp 349-67.

Teicher, M.D. (2000) 'Wounds that time won't heal: the neurobiology of child abuse', *Cerebrum: the Dana Forum on brain science*, vol 2, pp 50-67.

Teplin, L.A., Abram, K.M., McClelland, G.M., Dulcan, M.K. and Mericle, A.A. (2002) 'Psychiatric disorders in youth in juvenile detention', *Archives of General Psychiatry*, vol 59, pp 1133-43.

Troy, M. and Sroufe, L.A. (1987) 'Victimisation among preschoolers: role of attachment relationship history', *Journal of American Academy of Child and Adolescent Psychiatry*, vol 26, pp 166-72.

UNICEF (United Nations Children's Fund) (2003) *A league table of child maltreatment and deaths in rich nations*, Report Card 5, Innocenti Research Centre, Florence: UNICEF.

Van der Kolk, B.A. (1996) 'The body keeps the score: approaches to the psychobiology of post traumatic stress disorder', in B.A. Van der Kolk, A.C. McFarlane and L. Weisaeth (eds) *Traumatic stress: The effects of overwhelming experience on mind, body, and society* (pp 214-41), New York: Guilford Press.

Van der Kolk, B.A. (2005) 'Developmental trauma disorder', *Psychiatric Annals*, vol 35-5, May, pp 401-8.

Watt, G.C.M. (1996) 'All together now: why social deprivation matters to everyone', *British Medical Journal*, vol 312, pp 1026-9.

Weiler, B. and Widom, C.S. (1996) 'Psychopathy and violent behaviour in abused and neglected young adults', *Criminal Behaviour and Mental Health*, vol 6, pp 253-71.

Yehuda, R. (1997) 'Sensitisation of the hypothalamic-pituitary axis in post traumatic stress disorder', in R. Yehuda and A.C. McFarlane (eds) *Psychobiology of post traumatic stress disorder*, pp 157-82.

Yehuda, R., Halligan, S.L. and Bierer, L.M. (2002) 'Cortisol levels in adult offspring of Holocaust survivors: relation to PTSD symptom severity in the parent and the child', *Psychoneuroendocrinology*, vol 27, pp 171-80.

Yehuda, R., Engel, S.M., Brand, S., Seckl, J., Marcus, S.M. and Berkowitz, G.S. (2005) 'Transgenerational effects of post traumatic stress disorder in babies of mothers exposed to the World Trade Center attacks during pregnancy', *Journal of Clinical Endocrinology and Metabolism*, vol 90, pp 4115-8.

Zeitlin, S.D., McNally, R.J. and Cassidy, K.C. (1993) 'Alexithymia in victims of sexual assault: an effect of repeated traumatisation', *American Journal of Psychiatry*, vol 150, pp 661-3.

Zeitlin, S.D., Lane, R.D., O'Leary, D.S. and Schrift, M.K. (1989) 'Inter-hemispheric transfer deficit and alexithymia', *American Journal of Psychiatry*, vol 146, pp 1434-9.

Zulueta, F. de (1998) 'Human violence: a treatable epidemic', *Medicine, Conflict and Survival*, www.informaworld.com/smpp/title~content=t713673482~db=all~tab=i ssueslist~branches=14 - v1414, pp 46-55

Zulueta, F. de (1999) 'Borderline personality disorder as seen from an attachment perspective: a review', *Criminal Behaviour and Mental Health*, vol 9, pp 237-53.

Zulueta, F. de (2006a) 'The role of the traumatic attachment in the assessment and treatment of adults with a history of childhood abuse and neglect', *British Journal of Forensic Practice*, vol 8, no 3, pp 4-15 (www.pavpub.com/pavpub/journals/BJFP/thismonthssample.pdf).

Zulueta, F. de (2006b) *From pain to violence: The roots of human destructiveness* (2nd edition), Chichester: John Wiley and Sons.

Early intervention in the youth justice sphere: a knowledge-based critique

Barry Goldson

> When a youth commits a crime and we let him go, then the probability that he will do another crime is actually lower than if we'd punished him. (Von Liszt, 1893)

> [W]e have ensured that young offenders are now much more likely to be brought to justice through significant transformations to the Youth Justice System. (HM Government, 2008, para 2)

Introduction: 'risk', prevention and early intervention

In many respects, modes of intervention that ostensibly aim to prevent or ameliorate 'risk' play an increasingly significant role in shaping, defining and legitimising modern forms of child and youth governance. The multiple and fluid meanings routinely attached to the concept of 'risk', however, are not always clear. Some children and young people are conceived as being particularly *susceptible to 'risk'*, implying constructions of vulnerability and invoking the imperatives of protection and safeguarding (as in modern child welfare discourse; see, for example, DCSF, 2007). Conversely, different constituencies of the young are deemed to comprise a primary *source of 'risk'*, implying a threatening or menacing presence and invoking regulatory and corrective priorities (as in contemporary youth justice discourse; see, for example, HM Government, 2008).

Such binary conceptualisations inevitably tend to oversimplify (Goldson, 2004). Nonetheless, they each provide rationales for various forms of early intervention, greater levels of adult supervision, more intensive patterns of regulation and surveillance and, ultimately, circumscribed access to public spaces for children and young people. In the first instance, a variety of disparate factors − ranging from concerns regarding 'stranger-danger', predatory adults and paedophilia, through to the consequences of increasing road traffic, expanding car-dependent lifestyles, the diminishing quantity and quality of public facilities (parks, adventure playgrounds, youth clubs), the growth of home-based entertainment, organised indoor leisure activities and major developments in (and the proliferation of) information technology and communication systems − have combined to limit the visibility, activity and social interaction of children and young people in the public sphere. Alternatively, constructions of 'anti-social', disorderly and offending youth, together with an increasing array of dispersal powers, civil injunctions and criminal orders to which they have been exposed in recent years, have served to limit their movement, inhibit their public presence and subject them to greater levels of restriction, regulation and control. In this way – although underpinned by quite different and even contradictory rationales and objectives – the 'risk averse society' (Gill, 2007) has given rise to a 'culture of fear' (Furedi, 2002), be it fear *for* the young or fear *of* the young.

If notions of 'risk' per se tend to legitimise intensifying modes of child and youth governance, contemporary policy and practice discourses – with regard to child welfare and youth justice – emphasise *early intervention*, targeted, on the one hand, at potential, prospective and/or anticipated risks and, on the other hand, at actual, immediate and/or proven risks. In each case, benign constructions of prevention and amelioration are normally emphasised. In the child welfare domain, for example, as Munro (2007, p 41) has observed:

> At first sight, a policy of prevention and early intervention ... looks beguilingly altruistic. It has many persuasive attractions: it could reduce the amount of distress or harm experienced by the child [and] problems may be easier to tackle while they are still at a low level.

Similarly, with regard to youth justice, early intervention conveys a seductive commonsensical logic whereby 'risk assessments' are apparently premised on the basis that early identification of children and young people most likely to engage in 'anti-social', 'disorderly' and/or 'offending' behaviour allows for preventive intervention. In this sense, it is difficult to quarrel with policy and practice initiatives that claim to obviate the onset of distress, harm and/or problematic behaviours.

On closer inspection, however, whether in the child welfare realm (see, for example, Goldson, 2002; Peters and Barlow, 2003; Munro, 2004; Parton, 2006; Munro 2007) or the youth justice domain (see, for example, Goldson, 2000a; Kempf-Leonard and Peterson, 2000; Hughes and Follett, 2006; Smith, 2006), the logic and consequence of early intervention strategies are pitted with theoretical, conceptual and practical problems. This chapter engages with such problems as they specifically relate to the youth justice sphere and, by drawing on key sources of evidence in the space available, it aims to subject early intervention to knowledge-based critique.

Early intervention and the 'new youth justice'

As New Labour's youth justice policies evolved and developed throughout the 1990s, the emphasis on early – even pre-emptive – intervention consolidated (see, for example, Michael, 1993a, 1993b, 1993c; Labour Party, 1996; Straw and Anderson, 1996). Immediately prior to the 1997 General Election, Jack Straw and Alan Michael

– two of the principal architects of the 'new youth justice' (Goldson, 2000b) – claimed that:

> Insufficient attention is given to changing behaviour.... Too little is done to change youngsters' behaviour early in their offending career.... We believe that the time has come for fundamental changes to be made.... We have to start again ... by prioritising *early intervention* to nip offending in the bud. (Straw and Michael, 1996, passim, emphasis added)

Indeed, within months of coming to power, the first New Labour administration produced three key consultative documents (Home Office, 1997a, 1997b, 1997c), followed by a White Paper entitled *No more excuses: A new approach to tackling youth crime in England and Wales* (Home Office, 1997d). Early intervention was repeatedly emphasised throughout. Perhaps more significantly, two major pieces of legislation – the Crime and Disorder Act 1998 and the Youth Justice and Criminal Evidence Act 1999 – each gave statutory effect to interventionist priorities. The *No more excuses* White Paper was unequivocal:

> The trouble with the current cautioning system is that ... a caution does not result in any follow up action, so the opportunity is lost for *early intervention* to turn youngsters away from crime.... The Government feels that more radical action is now needed.... The Crime and Disorder Bill will abolish cautioning and replace it with a statutory police Reprimand and Final Warning scheme. Within a clear statutory framework the police will decide whether to Reprimand a young offender, give a Final Warning or bring criminal charges. When a Final Warning is given, this will usually be followed by a community intervention programme ... to address the causes of offending and so reduce the risk of further crime. (Home Office, 1997d, paras 5.10-5.12, emphasis added)

As signalled in the White Paper, sections 65 and 66 of the Crime and Disorder Act 1998 put an end to cautioning and introduced a statutory system of Reprimands and Final Warnings as key vehicles for implementing early intervention across the youth justice system. The Reprimand is targeted at children and young people who 'have not previously been convicted of an offence' (s 65(1)(d)). The Final Warning (a 'one-off' disposal unless at least two years have elapsed from the date of an earlier warning) is normally reserved for 'second-time offenders' (s 65(3)(b)), although the legislation also allows for a Final Warning to be issued instead of a Reprimand for a first offence where 'the constable ... considers the offence to be so serious as to require a warning' (s 65(4)). When a Final Warning is administered, the child/young person is routinely referred to the local Youth Offending Team (YOT) for a 'rehabilitation programme' assessment (s 66(1)). The legislation 'envisages that Final Warnings will usually be accompanied by an intervention programme' (YJB, 2004, para 6.1) and, in this way, it is claimed that 'by intervening early and effectively before crime becomes a habit, we can stop today's young offenders becoming tomorrow's career criminals' (Home Office, 1997a, para 47).

Furthermore, section 66(5) of the Crime and Disorder Act 1998 provides that Reprimands, Final Warnings and 'any report on a failure by a person to participate in a rehabilitation programme' (related to a Final Warning) 'may be cited in criminal proceedings in the same circumstances as a conviction'. The principal reasons for this were highlighted in an earlier consultation paper and are clearly designed to 'up-tariff' children and young people, allowing the courts to impose more intensive (punitive) forms of intervention in cases of further offending, particularly where a lack of compliance and/or cooperation is reported:

> [F]or the Final Warning to be effective in preventing re-offending, there must be sufficient incentive for young offenders and their parents to co-operate and complete the intervention programme ... further sanctions may be required ... any unreasonable non-compliance would be recorded on the individual's criminal record ... and that record might be taken into account by a court when sentencing for any subsequent offence. (Home Office, 1997a, paras 65-8)

If the Crime and Disorder Act 1998 has served to facilitate early intervention at the pre-court stage of the youth justice process, the Youth Justice and Criminal Evidence Act 1999 consolidates it within the court setting. Part 1 of the 1999 Act provides the Referral Order: the standard sentence imposed by the youth court, or other magistrates' court, for children and young people who have been convicted of an offence or offences for the *first time*. In such cases, the court normally refers the child/young person to a Youth Offender Panel (YOP). It is the function of such panels to establish a 'youth offender contract' (s 8(6)) with the young person, specifying conditions and a 'programme of behaviour' that they are obliged to observe. Section 8 of the Act identifies typical 'terms of the programme', including:

- financial or other forms of reparation to the victim/s of the offence/s;
- mediation sessions with the victim/s;
- unpaid work as a service to the community;
- conditions that require the child/young person to be at home at specified times and attend school or work;
- specified activities to 'address offending behaviour' and/or to serve rehabilitative purposes with respect to drug and/or alcohol misuse;
- reporting conditions to persons and/or places;
- prohibition from association with specified persons and/or places; and
- compliance with the supervision and recording requirements of the programme.

Once a 'programme of behaviour' has been established and a 'youth offender contract' has been signed by the young person (s 8(5)(b)), their 'progress' is subject to periodic review by the YOP (s 11).

The imperative of early intervention – initially signalled through a series of consultation papers in the early to mid 1990s, subsequently announced as a key youth justice policy objective in the *No more excuses* White Paper in 1997 and, ultimately, provided with statutory footing via the 1998 and 1999 Acts – remains a central plank of the 'new youth justice'. The Home Secretary, the Secretary of State for Children, Schools and Families and the Secretary of State for Justice and Lord Chancellor recently stated jointly:

> [W]e will address the root causes of crime ... in a much more targeted and individual way: spotting problems *early* and intervening to stop them getting out of control ... we will offer non-negotiable intervention ... backed by £100 million of extra funding to tackle this problem. (HM Government, 2008, p 1; emphasis added)

The enduring prominence of early intervention within contemporary youth justice discourse is curious, particularly given the government's claimed attachment to evidence-based policy formation. At the level of specificity, there is accumulating evidence to suggest that Reprimands and Final Warnings (see, for example, Bell et al, 1999; Goldson, 2000a; Evans and Puech, 2001; Bateman, 2002; Kemp et al, 2002; Holdaway, 2003; Holdaway and Desborough, 2004; Pragnell, 2005; Morgan and Newburn, 2007; Evans, 2008a; Nacro, 2008) and Referral Orders (see, for example, Wonnacott, 1999; Goldson, 2000a; Haines, 2000; Crawford, 2003; Crawford and Newburn, 2003) are problematic on a number of counts. It is not the intention here to present a micro-level evaluative analysis of specific interventions or statutory powers, however. Rather, the remainder of this chapter will engage a more generic critique of early intervention in the youth justice sphere, underpinned and informed by three intersecting core areas of knowledge.

Knowledge-based critique

The central argument advanced here is that early intervention in the youth justice sphere is counterintuitive; it often serves to intensify the very problems that it apparently seeks to resolve. It is a proposition derived from theoretical, conceptual and empirical bodies of knowledge. Such overlapping knowledges have evolved and developed over time and it is not practical in a chapter such as this to engage a comprehensive analysis. For present purposes, therefore, selected key elements of a wider knowledge base are presented and discussed. Taken together, they form the foundations on which a more complete critique of early intervention in contemporary youth justice might rest.

Theoretically derived critique

Theoretically derived critique of early intervention in the youth justice sphere is centrally informed by interactionist, social reaction and labelling perspectives, originally developed by social scientists working out of the University of Chicago from the mid-1930s onwards. The work of social psychologist, George Herbert Mead (1934), and sociologist, Herbert Blumer (1969), was pivotal in emphasising the significance of social interaction in the construction of the human 'self'. Put simply, Mead and Blumer argued that individuals essentially form their self-concepts (their 'selves') through processes of social interaction and reflexive awareness of how they are seen by others. Such insights were subsequently applied as a means of conceptualising responses to crime and deviance as *transactional processes*: the result of interactions between a person who commits an act (the 'offender') and those who respond to it (agents and agencies of social control/criminal justice). The nature of intervention and its impact –on both the 'offender's' sense of self and the social reactions to her/him from others – become key analytical variables.

In this way, such approaches depart from orthodox modes of positivist aetiological analysis. As Cohen (1967, p 121) observed:

> In the field of juvenile delinquency, for example, the bulk of research is directed towards the taxonomic tabulation of the delinquent's traits (or attitudes, or values) in an attempt to see how delinquents differ from non-delinquents. On this basis causal theories are constructed.

This is particularly evident in 'risk-factor' discourses, the logics of actuarialism and the pre-emptive and/or early modes of intervention that characterise contemporary youth justice. Interactionist perspectives, however, are less concerned with 'causal theories' predicated on 'risk factors' and more interested in the iatrogenic effect that (early) intervention and formal 'labelling' might impose. A starting point is the recognition that it is not uncommon for children and young people to transgress the law and the primary difference between those who are conceptualised as 'offenders' and those who are not is 'understood not as a difference in psychological character but as a consequence of whether or not the young person has become entangled in the criminal justice system' (Pearson, 1994, p 1186).

The relative 'normality' of youth crime is evidenced in a range of self-report studies that have consistently (over time) indicated that offending is not uncommon in adolescence (see, for example, Shapland, 1978; Graham and Bowling, 1995; Flood-Page et al, 2000; Budd et al, 2005; Wilson et al, 2006). Interactionist, labelling and social reaction theorists help us to understand the means by which formal interventions – particularly the processes of arrest, charge, prosecution, trial and sentence – serve to apply 'offender labels' to children and young people and, in so doing, confirm delinquent identities (Lemert, 1951; Kitsuse, 1962; Becker, 1963; Matza, 1964; Erikson, 1966; Lemert, 1967; Matza, 1969). Blackmore (1984, pp 45-6) explains:

> The labelling perspective is particularly relevant ... as it focuses specifically on how the process of social control can affect delinquent behaviour. Traditionally the agencies of social control (police, schools, social services, probation and courts) were viewed as passive responders to delinquency. In other words they were seen as merely reacting to delinquent behaviour. However, labelling theorists have questioned this

and instead focused attention on the ways that social control agencies react can in fact create and lead to further deviant behaviour.

In essence, the core proposition maintains that the application of stigmatising labels, followed by negative social reactions, is a routine consequence of (early) intervention. Furthermore, such processes produce 'outsiders' and this invariably invokes further and more intensive forms of targeted intervention. It follows that cycles of intervention 'create' (or at least consolidate and confirm) offender 'selves'. This led Edwin Lemert (1967, p v) to conclude:

> [O]lder sociology ... tended to rest heavily upon the idea that deviance leads to social control. I have come to believe that the reverse idea, i.e., that social control leads to deviance, is equally tenable and the potentially richer premise for studying deviance in modern society.

Similarly, David Matza (1969, p 80) reflected on the 'irony' that 'the very effort to prevent, intervene, arrest and "cure" persons ... precipitates or seriously aggravates the tendency society wishes to guard against'.

The principal value of such approaches is that they unsettle the otherwise taken-for-granted commonsensical assumptions that early intervention serves to prevent youth crime. Indeed, they imply quite the opposite. Furthermore, questions relating to discretionary judgements, 'risk assessments', professional licence and, ultimately, power relations become key. Why are some 'categories' of children and young people (the poor and structurally disadvantaged) more likely than others to be 'labelled'? Why do labels 'stick' to particular constituencies of the young but not to others? In what ways do processes of criminalisation derive from, and compound, social injustices? What is the significance of social class, 'race', ethnicity and/or gender in comprehending differential patterns of labelling and negative social reaction? How do micro-social contexts and individualised processes connect with wider inequalities in structural power?

Such questions extend significantly beyond abstract theorisation. The implications for youth justice policy and practice in particular, and social policy and the behaviour of state agencies more generally, are considerable. Indeed, variants of interactionist, labelling and social reaction analyses provoke fundamental challenges to the rationales and practical effects of early intervention. This is not to deny the objective reality of youth crime. Neither should it be taken to imply that nothing should, or could, be done to address it. Rather, such theoretically derived critique serves to question the legitimacy of early intervention in the youth justice sphere and to query its political rationales, ethical foundations and practical consequences.

Conceptually derived critique

Dominant conceptual assumptions within contemporary policy discourse – particularly pertaining to complex contradictions in the social order, questions of responsibility, the role of state agencies and the criminal (youth) justice apparatus – are central to the critique of early intervention.

The children and young people who are most acutely targeted by way of early intervention are invariably drawn from the most damaged, distressed and neglected families, neighbourhoods and communities. This is not to imply essentialist positivism or to suggest that *all* poor children are troublesome, or that *only* poor children are refractory, but the intersections of chronic socioeconomic disadvantage, youth crime, processes of criminalisation and state intervention are long established (see, for example, Box, 1987). It is no coincidence, therefore, that poverty is the unifying social characteristic of the majority of young 'offenders'. While it would not be entirely accurate to suggest that contemporary youth justice policy and practice completely overlooks material conditions, its gaze is primarily fixed at the level of individual and/or familial circumstance. To put it another way, the perceived remedy for 'anti-social behaviour', disorder and/or crime is primarily harnessed to notions of individual responsibility as distinct from wider social–structural relations. Thus, individually targeted intervention, as distinct from universal generic services, tends to be the favoured 'modern' approach.

Indeed, the concept of 'risk' is routinely coupled with pathological constructions of wilful irresponsibility and individual failure (Goldson and Jamieson, 2002). The passport to statutory services, therefore, is essentially defined along purely negative lines. In order to 'qualify', in order to be offered a service – or perhaps, more accurately, to be 'targeted' by an 'intervention' – children, young people and their families must be seen to have 'failed' or be 'failing', to be 'posing risk', to be 'threatening' (either actually or potentially). In this way, conceptualisations of universal services recede into narrowing contexts of classification, control and correction where interventions are specifically targeted at those deemed to comprise the 'criminal', the 'near criminal', the 'possibly criminal', the 'sub-criminal', the 'anti-social' and/or the 'disorderly'.

A key practical consequence of the (mis)conceptualisations – or, to borrow Gouldner's (1970) term, 'domain assumptions' – that underpin 'risk'-based modes of early intervention is the distortion of core jurisprudential principles. In this sense, guilt is no longer the founding principle. Indeed, intervention can be triggered without any offence being committed, premised instead on a condition, a character or a lifestyle that is adjudged to be 'failing' or posing 'risk'. This represents a radical departure from conventional applications of youth justice that require first, publicly specified offences and second, guilt and responsibility proven in accordance with transparent codes of evidence, fact and law. The same applications involve an open trial in a court of law, clearly defined safeguards in the form of defence and legal representation/advocacy and access to review and appeal procedures. In contrast, modes of risk classification and early intervention are unencumbered by long-established principles such as 'the burden of proof', 'beyond reasonable doubt' and 'due legal process'. Instead, intervention is triggered by assessment, discretionary judgement and the spurious logic of prediction and actuarialism. It follows that intervention becomes less a matter of transparent justice and more a question of opaque administrative and professional process. Children and young people face judgement, and are exposed to criminalising labelling and modes of intervention, not only on the basis of what they *have* done, but what they *might* do, who they are or who they are thought to be.

This not only negates fundamental principles of justice; it also violates international human rights standards (Goldson and Muncie, 2006, p 97). Furthermore, the crude, slavish and mechanistic application of 'risk assessments' within youth justice practice is actually premised on fundamental misconceptions of the 'evidence base' (Case, 2007; Kemshall, 2008). Indeed, there is little, if any, substantial evidence that 'risk factor' assessments can accurately predict and identify future young offenders. Thus, Carole Sutton and her colleagues, paradoxically among the keenest and most prominent advocates of the early intervention 'risk factor' paradigm, counsel the need for 'caution':

> In particular, any notion that better screening can enable policy makers to identify young children destined to join the 5 per cent of offenders responsible for 50-60 per cent of crime is fanciful. Even if there were no ethical objections to putting 'potential delinquent' labels round the necks of young children, there would continue to be statistical barriers. Research into the continuity of anti-social behaviour shows substantial flows out of – as well as in to – the pool of children who develop chronic conduct problems. This demonstrates the dangers of assuming that anti-social five year olds are the criminals or drug abusers of tomorrow.... (Sutton et al, 2004, p 5)

There are indeed strong grounds for querying the conceptual rationales that underpin recent policy and practice initiatives, such as Youth Inclusion and Support Panels (YISPs) that seek to 'identify' the 'most at risk 7-13 year olds' and engage them in 'programmes' (Home Office, 2004, p 41). Equally, practices of coercive 'early intervention to address criminal-type anti-social behaviour in children under 10 (the age of criminal responsibility) where a voluntary approach has not worked' (Home Office, 2004, p 42) and, more recently, the seemingly oxymoronic 'offer of non-negotiable intervention for families at greatest risk of offending' (HM Government, 2008, p 1) – literally an 'offer' that cannot be refused – are based on profoundly questionable conceptualisations.

Empirically derived critique

Empirically derived critique of early intervention tends to take two forms. What we might call *positive critique* rests on a body of knowledge that suggests that diversionary strategies – which aim to avoid criminogenic labelling, limit intervention to the necessary minimum and deliberately restrict young people's formal engagement with justice agencies – neutralise iatrogenic consequences and allow for the effective management of youth justice systems (Haines and Drakeford, 1998). On the other hand, *negative critique* is informed by, and builds on, a developing corpus of empirical research that reveals the damaging and counterproductive tendencies of early intervention.

Up until the sweeping reforms and policy U-turns of the mid to late 1990s, the deployment of informal warnings and cautions – as distinct from formal prosecution and court appearance – was standard practice. Indeed, two particularly important Home Office Circulars – 14/1985 and 59/1990 – actively promoted the use of such *diversionary* measures (Home Office, 1985, 1990). Home Office Circular 14/1985, as Muncie (1999, p 272) notes, 'encouraged the use of informal warnings' to divert children and young people from the justice process without activating formal criminal records. The practice of issuing informal warnings was such that the Audit Commission (1996, p 20) estimated that 'around 10% of young offenders identified by the police … are now warned'. Finally, Home Office Circular 59/1990 stated that the purpose of cautioning was to deal quickly and simply with less serious offenders, divert them from court and to reduce the likelihood of reoffending.

The practical effect of the two Home Office Circulars and the development of strategic diversionary practice was not insignificant. Gibson and Cavadino (1995, p 56) observed that the number of offenders cautioned doubled between 1985 and 1995, while Gelsthorpe and Morris (1999, p 210) reported that 'most children who offended over this period were diverted by the police: 90 per cent of boys and 97 per cent of girls in 1993'. Evans (2008b, p 147) highlights the pragmatic grounds for pursuing such practice: 'diversion is cost effective, proportionate and works in the sense that young people who are cautioned are less likely to be reconvicted than those who are prosecuted'. The most effective diversionary strategy, however, is literally to remove children and young people from the reach of the youth justice system altogether by significantly raising the age of criminal responsibility. There are strong empirical grounds to support this proposition, not least evidence from jurisdictions where the age of criminal responsibility is substantially higher than it is in England and Wales and where 'it can be shown that there are no negative consequences to be seen in terms of crime rates' (Dunkel, 1996, p 38).

If 'positive critique' of early intervention is rooted in the *effectiveness* of diversionary strategies, 'negative critique' centres upon the correlative failings of interventionist approaches. Building on a body of earlier work (see, for example, Thorpe et al, 1980; Rutherford, 1986), recent empirical research has concluded that 'the key to reducing offending lies in minimal intervention and maximum diversion' (McAra and McVie, 2007, p 315). Indeed, drawing on their longitudinal programme of research on pathways into and out of offending for a cohort of 4,300 children and young people in Edinburgh and informed more broadly by a growing body of international studies,

McAra and McVie (2007, pp 337, 340) provide compelling empirical evidence of the problematic nature of early intervention:

> Doing less rather than more in individual cases may mitigate the potential for damage that system contact brings ... targeted early intervention strategies ... are likely to widen the net.... Greater numbers of children will be identified as at risk and early involvement will result in constant recycling into the system.... As we have shown, forms of diversion ... without recourse to formal intervention ... are associated with desistance from serious offending. Such findings are supportive of a maximum diversion approach.... Accepting that, in some cases, doing less is better than doing more requires both courage and vision on the part of policy makers.... To the extent that systems appear to damage young people and inhibit their capacity to change, then they do not, and never will, deliver justice.

Concluding thoughts

Since the election of the first New Labour government in 1997, the logics of diversion and minimum necessary intervention have been effectively expunged and replaced with polar opposite rationales, policies and practices: early (even pre-emptive) intervention. This trend runs counter to the directions signalled by theoretical, conceptual and empirical knowledges and, as such, it defies criminological rationality. Despite the rhetoric of evidence-based approaches to policy formation and practice development, however, the driving force behind much youth justice reform over the previous decade ultimately descends from populist punitiveness and short-term political calculations. Accordingly, the youth justice apparatus has expanded on an industrial scale and early intervention has given rise to substantial net-widening. Indeed, the fourfold combination of, first, new powers, procedures and practices – most notably Reprimands, Final Warnings and Referral Orders (as discussed above), second, new police targets relating to 'offences brought to justice' and 'sanction detection' (Morgan and Newburn, 2007; Bateman, 2008), third, the conflation of 'anti-social behaviour', 'disorder' and 'crime' (Goldson, 2005) and, fourth, the development of 'risk'-based modalities and 'pre-crime' interventions (Smith, 2008) have produced a bloated and obese youth justice system.

In August 2007, the Youth Justice Board's annual report was published. The report refers to 'missing data for 2005/06' but, despite this, the available statistics reveal that in a single year no fewer than 97,329 children 'entered' the youth justice system in England and Wales for the 'first time' (YJB, 2007, p 23). In July 2008, the Board's 2007-08 report was published and, based on projected figures, it anticipates a further 89,525 'first time entrants' being drafted into the youth justice system during the year under review (YJB, 2008, p 23). Perhaps more problematically, the interventionist 'ratcheting-up' effect is not confined to the front end of the system. As Morgan and Newburn (2007, pp 1046-7) have observed:

> [T]he pattern is clear. Young offenders are today more likely to be criminalised and subject to a greater level of intervention than before the 1998 reforms. If dealt with pre-court their warning is more likely to be accompanied by an intervention. They are more likely to be prosecuted. If convicted they are less likely to receive a discharge or fine. If subject to a community sentence it is more likely to be onerous. And last but not least ... the number of children and young people sentenced to custody is still 35% higher than a few years before the 1998 [Crime and Disorder] Act.

This is neither coincidence nor accident. Ultimately, early intervention and custodial detention are inextricably linked along a continuum that has no legitimate claim to criminological rationality.

References

Audit Commission (1996) *Misspent youth: Young people and crime*, London: The Audit Commission.

Bateman, T. (2002) 'Living with Final Warnings: making the best of a bad job?', *Youth Justice*, 2, pp 131-40.

Bateman, T. (2008) 'Further increases in the number of children processed by the youth justice system in England and Wales', *Youth Justice*, 8, pp 82-3.

Becker, H. (1963) *Outsiders: Studies in the sociology of deviance*, New York: Free Press.

Bell, A., Hodgson, M. and Pragnell, S. (1999) 'Diverting children and young people from crime and the criminal justice system', in B. Goldson (ed) *Youth justice: Contemporary policy and practice*, Aldershot: Ashgate.

Blackmore, J. (1984) 'Delinquency theory and practice: a link through IT', *Youth and Policy*, 9.

Blumer, H. (1969) *Symbolic interactionism*, Englewood Cliffs, NJ: Prentice-Hall.

Box, S. (1987) *Recession, crime and punishment*, Basingstoke: Macmillan.

Budd, T., Sharp, C., Weir, G., Wilson, D. and Owen, N. (2005) *Young people and crime: Findings from the 2004 Offending, Crime and Justice Survey*, Home Office Statistical Bulletin 20/05, London: Home Office.

Case, S. (2007) 'Questioning the "evidence" of risk that underpins evidence-led youth justice interventions', *Youth Justice*, 7, pp 91-105.

Cohen, S. (1967) 'Mods, rockers and the rest: community reactions to juvenile delinquency', *Howard Journal*, 12, pp 121-30.

Crawford, A. (2003) '"Contractual governance" of deviant behaviour', *Journal of Law and Society*, 4, pp 479-505.

Crawford, A. and Newburn, T. (2003) *Youth offending and restorative justice: Implementing reform in youth justice*, Cullompton: Willan.

DCSF (Department for Children, Schools and Families) (2007) *The children's plan: Building brighter futures*, London: DCSF.

Dunkel, F. (1996) 'Current directions in criminal policy', in W. McCarney (ed) *Juvenile delinquents and young people in danger in an open environment*, Winchester: Waterside Books.

Erikson, K. (1966) *Wayward puritans: A study in the sociology of deviance*, New York: Wiley.

Evans, R. (2008a) 'Reprimands and Final Warnings', in B. Goldson (ed) *Dictionary of youth justice*, Cullompton: Willan.

Evans, R. (2008b) 'Diversion', in B. Goldson (ed) *Dictionary of youth justice*, Cullompton: Willan.

Evans, R. and Puech, K. (2001) 'Warnings and Reprimands: popular punitiveness or restorative justice?', *Criminal Law Review*, October, pp 794-805.

Flood-Page, C., Campbell, S., Harrington, V. and Miller, J. (2000) *Youth crime: Findings from the 1998/99 Youth Lifestyles Survey*, Home Office Research Study No 209, London: Home Office.

Furedi, F. (2002) *Culture of fear: Risk taking and the morality of low expectation* (2nd edition), London: Continuum.

Gelsthorpe, L. and Morris, A. (1999) 'Much ado about nothing – a critical comment on key provisions relating to children in the Crime and Disorder Act 1998', *Child and Family Law Quarterly*, 11, pp 209-21.

Gibson, B. and Cavadino, P. (1995) *Criminal justice process*, Winchester: Waterside Press.

Gill, T. (2007) *No fear: Growing up in a risk averse society*, London: Calouste Gulbenkian Foundation.

Goldson, B. (2000a) 'Wither diversion? Interventionism and the new youth justice', in B. Goldson (ed) *The new youth justice*, Lyme Regis: Russell House.

Goldson, B. (ed) (2000b) *The new youth justice*, Lyme Regis: Russell House.

Goldson, B. (2002) 'New Labour, social justice and children: political calculation and the deserving–undeserving schism', *The British Journal of Social Work*, 32, pp 683-95.

Goldson, B. (2004) 'Victims or threats? Children, care and control', in J. Fink (ed) *Care: Personal lives and social policy*, Bristol: The Policy Press in association with The Open University.

Goldson, B. (2005) 'Taking liberties: policy and the punitive turn', in H. Hendrick (ed) *Children and social policy: An essential reader*, Bristol: The Policy Press.

Goldson, B. and Jamieson, J. (2002) 'Youth crime, the "parenting deficit" and state intervention: a contextual critique', *Youth Justice*, 2, pp 82-99.

Goldson, B. and Muncie, J. (2006) 'Rethinking youth justice: comparative analysis, international human rights and research evidence', *Youth Justice*, 6, pp 91-106.

Gouldner, A. (1970) *The coming crisis of Western sociology*, London: Heinemann.

Graham, J. and Bowling, B. (1995) *Young people and crime*, Home Office Research Study No 145, London: Home Office.

Haines, K. (2000) 'Referral Orders and Youth Offender Panels: restorative approaches and the new youth justice', in B. Goldson (ed) *The new youth justice*, Lyme Regis: Russell House.

Haines, K. and Drakeford, M. (1998) *Young people and youth justice*, Basingstoke: Macmillan.

HM Government (2008) *Youth crime action plan 2008*, London: COI.

Holdaway, S. (2003) 'The Final Warning: appearance and reality', *Criminal Justice*, 3, pp 351-67.

Holdaway, S. and Desborough, S. (2004) *Final Warning projects: The national evaluation of the Youth Justice Board's Final Warning projects*, London: YJB.

Home Office (1985) *The cautioning of offenders*, Circular 14/1985, London: Home Office.

Home Office (1990) *The cautioning of offenders*, Circular 59/90, London: Home Office.

Home Office (1997a) *Tackling youth crime: A consultation paper*, London: Home Office.

Home Office (1997b) *Tackling delays in the youth justice system: A consultation paper*, London: Home Office.

Home Office (1997c) *New national and local focus on youth crime: A consultation paper*, London: Home Office.

Home Office (1997d) *No more excuses: A new approach to tackling youth crime in England and Wales*, London: Home Office.

Home Office (2004) *Confident communities in a secure Britain: The Home Office strategic plan 2004-08*, London: The Stationery Office.

Hughes, G. and Follett, M. (2006) 'Community safety, youth and the "anti-social"', in B. Goldson and J. Muncie (eds) *Youth crime and justice: Critical issues*, London: Sage Publications.

Kemp, V., Sorsby, A., Liddle, M. and Merrington, S. (2002) *Assessing responses to youth offending in Northamptonshire*, Research Briefing 2, London: Nacro.

Kempf-Leonard, K. and Peterson, E. (2000) 'Expanding realms of the new penology: the advent of actuarial justice for juveniles', *Punishment and Society*, 2, pp 66-97.

Kemshall, H. (2008) 'Risks, rights and justice: understanding and responding to youth risk', *Youth Justice*, 8, pp 21-37.

Kitsuse, J. (1962) 'Societal reaction to deviant behaviour', *Social Problems*, 9, pp 247-56.

Labour Party (1996) *Tackling youth crime, reforming youth justice: A consultation paper on an agenda for change*, London: Labour Party.

Lemert, E. (1951) *Social pathology*, New York: McGraw Hill.

Lemert, E. (1967) *Human deviance, social problems and social control*, Englewood Cliffs, NJ: Prentice Hall.

Matza, D. (1964) *Delinquency and drift*, New York: Wiley.

Matza, D. (1969) *Becoming deviant*, Englewood Cliffs, NJ: Prentice Hall.

McAra, L. and McVie, S. (2007) 'Youth justice? The impact of system contact on patterns of desistance from offending', *European Journal of Criminology*, 4, pp 315-45.

Mead, G.H. (1934) *Mind, self and society*, Chicago, IL: University of Chicago Press.

Michael, A. (1993a) *Getting a grip on youth crime*, London: Labour Party.

Michael, A. (1993b) *Tackling crime*, London: Labour Party.

Michael, A. (1993c) *Getting a grip on youth crime: A proposal for earlier, effective action*, London: Labour Party.

Morgan, R. and Newburn, T. (2007) 'Youth justice', in M. Maguire, R. Morgan and R. Reiner (eds) *The Oxford handbook of criminology*, Oxford: Oxford University Press.

Muncie, J. (1999) *Youth and crime: A critical introduction*, London: Sage Publications.

Munro, E. (2004) 'A simpler way to understand the results of risk assessment instruments', *Children and Youth Services Review*, 26, pp 877-87.

Munro, E. (2007) 'Confidentiality in a preventive child welfare system', *Ethics and Social Welfare*, 1, pp 41-55.

Nacro (National Association for the Care and Resettlement of Offenders) (2008) *Youth crime briefing: Some facts about children and young people who offend – 2006*, London: Nacro.

Parton, N. (2006) *Safeguarding childhood: Early intervention and surveillance in a late modern society*, Basingstoke: Palgrave Macmillan.

Pearson, G. (1994) 'Youth, crime and society', in M. Maguire, R. Morgan and R. Reiner (eds) *The Oxford handbook of criminology*, Oxford: Clarendon Press.

Peters, R. and Barlow, J. (2003) 'Systematic review of instruments designed to predict child maltreatment during the antenatal and postnatal periods', *Child Abuse Review*, 12, pp 416-39.

Pragnell, S. (2005) 'Reprimands and Final Warnings', in T. Bateman and J. Pitts (eds) *The RHP companion to youth justice*, Lyme Regis: Russell House Publishing.

Rutherford, A. (1986) *Growing out of crime*, London: Penguin.

Shapland, J. (1978) 'Self-reported delinquency in boys aged 11 to 14', *British Journal of Criminology*, 18, pp 255-66.

Smith, R. (2006) 'Actuarialism and early intervention in contemporary youth justice', in B. Goldson and J. Muncie (eds) *Youth crime and justice: Critical issues*, London: Sage Publications.

Smith, R. (2008) 'Actuarialism', in B. Goldson (ed) *Dictionary of youth justice*, Cullompton: Willan.

Straw, J. and Anderson, J. (1996) *Parenting*, London: Labour Party.

Straw, J. and Michael, A. (1996) *Tackling the causes of crime: Labour's proposals to prevent crime and criminality*, London: Labour Party.

Sutton, C., Utting, D. and Farrington, D. (2004) *Support from the start: Working with young children and their families to reduce the risks of crime and anti-social behaviour*, Research Brief 524, March, London: DfES.

Thorpe, D., Smith, D., Green, C. and Paley, J. (1980) *Out of care: The community support of juvenile offenders*, London: George Allen & Unwin.

Von Liszt, F. (1893) 'Die Deterministischen Gegner der Zweckstrafe' ('Deterministic Opponents of Purposive Punishment'), cited in M. Nagel (2008) *Media images of (youthful) offenders: a comparative analysis of race, class, gender in Germany and the United States*, Paper presented at the International Conference on Penal Abolition XII, King's College London, July.

Wilson, D., Sharp, C. and Patterson, A. (2006) *Young people and crime: Findings from the 2005 Offending Crime and Justice Survey*, London: Home Office.

Wonnacott, C. (1999) 'New legislation: the counterfeit contract – reform, pretence and muddled principles in the new referral order', *Child and Family Law Quarterly*, 11, pp 271-87.

YJB (Youth Justice Board) (2004) *National standards for youth justice services*, London: YJB.

YJB (2007) *Annual report and accounts 2006/07*, London: YJB.

YJB (2008) *Annual report and accounts 2007/08*, London: YJB.

European perspectives on prevention

Rob Allen

International norms

International norms have increasingly emphasised the importance of seeking to prevent young people's involvement in delinquency rather than simply addressing such behaviour after it happens. The United Nations (UN) Committee on the Rights of the Child has stated that 'a juvenile justice policy without a set of measures aimed at preventing juvenile delinquency suffers serious shortcomings' (UNCRC, 2007, p 7). The UN Guidelines for the prevention of juvenile delinquency (the Riyadh Guidelines) stress that 'prevention requires efforts on the part of the entire society to ensure the harmonious development of adolescents ... from early childhood' (UN, 1990, principle 2) and calls for close interdisciplinary cooperation. The role of the wider family, school, neighbourhood and peer group is also emphasised in the Council of Europe's recommendation 2003: 20 concerning 'new ways of dealing with juvenile delinquency and the role of juvenile justice' (Council of Europe, 2003).

The case for prevention is at one level self-evident, and there is still widespread support in Europe for Franz von Liszt's (1905) dictum that the best crime policy is social policy. Comparing data from the United Nations Children's Fund (UNICEF) against the prison population shows that countries that rank highly on child well-being tend to have lower rates of imprisonment than those who fare badly. Of the 10 countries in the study with the highest overall ranking for child well-being, seven have prison populations of less than 80 per 100,000, including Norway and all the Nordic countries. Of the bottom 10, six, including the UK1, have prison populations of over 100 per 100,000 (Allen, 2008) (see Figure 7.1).

International standards also contain some warnings about the potentially harmful consequences of early intervention. For example, the Riyadh Guidelines state that 'labelling a young person as deviant, delinquent or pre-delinquent often contributes to the development of a consistent pattern of undesirable behaviour' (UN, 1990, para 5f), and therefore suggest that '[f]ormal agencies of social control should only be utilized as a means of last resort'.

Figure 7.1: Dimensions of child well-being and prison population rate in OECD countries[1]

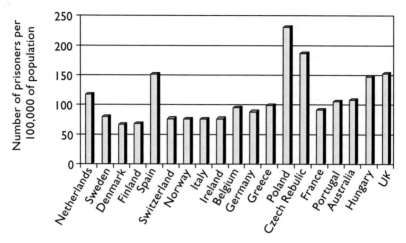

Note: [1] Countries in order of average rank for six dimensions of child well-being in UNICEF (2007)

Source: ICPS World Prison Brief

This is perhaps one reason why the Council of Europe's Human Rights Commissioner has expressed concern about Anti-Social Behaviour Orders (ASBOs), suggesting that their excessive use 'is more likely to exacerbate anti-social behaviour and crime amongst youths than effectively prevent it' (OHCHR, 2005, p 36). Although in his review of juvenile justice, he was enthusiastic about many of the preventive programmes introduced in England and Wales, he concluded that:

> [T]hese welcome initiatives have been significantly undermined by the introduction of a series of civil orders aimed at reducing urban nuisance, but whose primary effect has been to bring a whole range of persons, predominantly the young, within the scope of the criminal justice system and, often enough, behind bars without necessarily having committed a recognisable criminal offence. (OHCHR, 2005, p 27)

Crime prevention and social welfare

The age of criminal responsibility in England and Wales is uncommonly low: in most European countries, responding to children at risk of or involved in delinquency is much more centrally a matter for the social welfare authorities than in the UK. It is difficult to assess how delinquent children are dealt with by child welfare systems because data do not usually distinguish between the various reasons for referral. Finland is typical of Scandinavian countries where youth crime is not seen as a separate phenomenon that requires the construction of a programme specifically to combat it. Young people's problems are basically social problems, of which criminal activities are an indicator (Kuuire, 2003). In Austria, any prevention activities are covered by the 1989 Youth Welfare Act (Hazel, 2008). Indeed, one German commentator has suggested that a problem with the term 'crime prevention measures' to describe tried-and-tested provisions for leisure activity is that the new label makes potential criminals of all children who take part in service activities out of a desire for adventure (understandable at their age) or because they lack other opportunities (Schäfer, 2004, p 5).

There are important differences too in the way in which other countries seek to meet the needs of children. In continental Europe, the term 'pedagogy' or 'social pedagogy' is commonly used to describe a broad set of services for children, including 'childcare and early years, youth work, family support services, secure units for young offenders, residential care and play work' (Petrie et al, 2008, p 3). This model incorporates a much greater commitment to professional training and affords to practitioners a substantially higher status than that which is enjoyed by social work in the UK.

Notwithstanding the importance of these kinds of structural questions, the bulk of this chapter looks at specific programmes that focus on (a) families, (b) schools and (c) the community. The examples draw heavily on an excellent review of good practice in preventing juvenile crime across the European Union (Stevens et al, 2006) and a piece of comparative research undertaken for the Youth Justice Board (YJB) by Hazel (2008).

Family programmes

In Sweden, work with children under the age of criminal responsibility has included functional family therapy (FFT) and multidimensional treatment foster care (Utting et al, 2007). The Strengthening Families Programme has also been introduced, which is a family skills training programme to increase resilience and reduce risk factors for problem behaviours in six- to eleven-year-olds. An example of FFT is a project carried out in Bergsjon, a deprived district in Gothenburg. The family services unit responsible for investigations carries out the work for children and young people from birth to age 21, under the governance of the 1980 Swedish Welfare Act (SOL) and 1980 Special Provisions for the Care of Young People Act (LVU). A special project called 'Turning Point' was started in 2004, aimed at children reported for a crime for the first time because ordinary social services did not have the capacity to work with the children. Initially financed by the Swedish National Council for Crime Prevention, the project was due to become part of ordinary social services in 2006. The project makes contact at the police station when a child is arrested. The approach of the therapeutic involvement, which is entirely voluntary, is to empower the parents to help their children through a series of discussions. Of the 78 children involved in the first two years of the project, 25 were under the age of 13. Offences committed were predominantly shop theft and assault but included six cases of robbery. Eight children in the caseload had been known to reoffend (Larsson, 2005).

Interventions involving parents are increasingly common across Europe, with projects including EFFEKT in Germany, KOMET in Sweden and the Webster Stratton approach used in the UK. In France, there are parent centres providing assistance to families, and Germany has experimented with short-term residential support for families with follow-up: the Integrative Family Support model developed by Caritas, using a 'coaching model'.

Several countries have seen the development of multi-systemic therapy (MST) over the last five years, and indeed several Youth Offending Teams (YOTs) across England have integrated MST into their work (Cambridgshire, Reading). In Norway, a replication of the MST model developed in the US is funded by the Ministry of Children and the municipalities and coordinated by the University of Oslo (Ogden and Halliday-Boykins, 2004).

There is also a growing use of early years screening for behavioural risk factors in young children (for example, in Holland and Germany) (Hazel, 2008).

Education programmes

The second setting for programmes for disruptive children is educational, with activities falling into three categories: first, the use of schools to respond to emerging problems; second, enhanced programmes for use by teachers; and third, the deployment of police officers in educational settings. Such programmes need to be seen within the context of varying levels of provision for children with special educational needs and efforts to reduce levels of truancy and exclusion.

Some countries have continued to see the prevention of delinquency as part of a generic educational function. In Finland, where school is compulsory from age seven, it is the school health services and the student welfare team who are responsible for the pupils' well-being, with referral to special services or child protection when different forms of disturbance become apparent. Internal school welfare and support systems are the most significant forms of preventive social work for children of this age.

Among the specific programmes for teachers and other educators to use in the prevention of delinquency perhaps the best known is Olweus' Bullying Prevention Programme, widely used in Norway, Germany and elsewhere (Olweus, 1993; Olweus and Limber, 1999). This violence prevention and intervention programme is directed at so-called bullies who torment, mob or exhibit aggressive behaviour or violence towards peers, put them under pressure or steal from them. The programme targets three levels: the whole school, classrooms and individual pupils. School-wide measures include closer supervision during break periods, classroom initiatives that comprise the development of rules through classroom meetings, and options at the individual level that include discussions with particular pupils involved in incidents, the notification of the parents of the perpetrators and the holding of a meeting with the parties involved, which can involve entire classrooms. The adoption of a clear set of procedures, a victim focus and an approach that makes incidents public have helped victims become confident that a 'cry for help' will prompt consistent and resolute action by the school. Evaluation of the programmes in various settings has found reductions in direct forms of bullying, tangible and measurable improvements in the social climate at the school, and organisational changes such as new rules for break periods and a redesign of the area used during break periods (Olweus, 1995).

Baldry and Farrington (2007) recently reviewed anti-bullying programmes in schools in many different countries and found that, out of 16 evaluations, eight showed desirable results, two showed mixed results and four produced small or negligible results. Other programmes developed for use in schools include mediation to reduce violence. In Germany, the programme is targeted at pupils aged 9 to 12 with an aim of discovering what is at the root of interpersonal conflicts, learning to change negative reactions and improve social relationships, helping young people recognise and name their emotions, and familiarising students with conflicts without dramatising them. Students are put in groups of four by teachers and specially trained mediators, and take part in four-hour workshops once a week. During this time, they role-play and participate in other exercises that allow them to gain a deeper understanding of the emotions that are experienced during conflict.

Schools in many countries have developed life-skill training with an emphasis on avoiding delinquency and resolving conflicts peacefully. Skill-based training programmes include the 'Lions Quest' (www.lions-quest.org) from the US, which is known in Germany as 'Eigenstaendig Werden' or 'Becoming Autonomous'. The Skills for Growing programme is aimed at students in primary schools (Years 1 to 6) to prevent involvement in drugs and violent crime. The specific aims are to enhance social and life competencies as well as autonomy, to support the development of socially and emotionally sensible behaviour and to enhance conflict-resolution abilities. Teachers receive special training and incorporate this programme into the curriculum (42 lessons for Years 1 to 4 and 21 for Years 5 and 6). In the beginning, the subject matter is general, but as the students get older they begin to learn about specific topics such as bullying and stress reduction. Parts of the programme involve role-play and theatre, as well as meditation and relaxation workshops. In addition, work is done with parents to support the programme. In a quasi-experimental evaluation, the conflict-solving competencies, empathetic behaviour and communication skills of students in the experimental group were higher than those in the control group (Wibord and Hamewinkel, 2005), but no information appears to be available on whether the programme had an impact on disruptive or delinquent child behaviours.

The Skills for Growing programme is similar to Social Emotional Learning, another US model aimed at reducing delinquency, drug use and school exclusion (Stevens et al, 2006). The programme, which is being made available in Sweden, involves structured exercises for pupils to teach them self-awareness, empathy, the handling of emotions and social skills. Teachers and other school personnel also receive training, as do parents, who are provided with information so that they are able to help and encourage their child to learn. Pupils also take part in role-play, modelling and positive reinforcement, with opportunities to test new skills in different situations. A similar programme has been introduced in Norway. For example, the *'Lev Vel'* ('Live Well') teaching package was sent to all 3,335 schools in Norway by the Crime Prevention Council. In Austria, a module on 'communication, cooperation and conflict resolution' is taught in a set lesson every week (Hazel, 2008).

In some countries, schools are looking beyond the socioeducational approach to prevent crime. In Germany, as indeed in England through the Safer Schools Initiative, the police have now become more active in schools, where they have always been involved in traffic education schemes but have recently started to play a broader role (Stevens et al, 2006). The School Adoption Plan, in which police teach 12 classes in primary school, is operated in a number of countries (Hazel, 2008).

Community programmes

The third constellation of programmes focuses on the community. Examples include various restorative justice approaches. Norway's child welfare law allows restorative justice, overseen by a national network of mediation boards, for those under the age of criminal responsibility. In Germany, the youth services have begun to employ reparation of damage done, seeing it as a successful way of helping children to appreciate the cause-and-effect aspects of their delinquent acts.

The Neighbourhood Tutors project in Portugal, which takes a rather different approach, seeks to work with children and adolescents from immigrant and minority ethnic families (6- to 18-year-olds). Effectively, this is a mentoring programme focused on young people involved in disruptive and delinquent behaviours. The aim of the work is fairly conventional: to support social inclusion; decrease truancy and early school leaving; promote cognitive, social and personal competencies; and support more efficient parental guidance through family and community involvement in school dynamics. The method, however, is innovative in that it chooses a group of young people at risk and trains them to be neighbourhood tutors, who work with selected young people and link school, family and community. The tutors are then integrated into schools along with a psychologist and social worker. Through the use of pedagogical activities, organised sports, leisure time and psychological intervention, the programme aims to tackle social exclusion.

In similar vein, a Berlin scheme, originally aimed at Bosnian Roma children, developed provisions that successfully involved children who are normally extremely difficult to reach. *'Fallschirm'* ('Parachute') was established in 1998 as a community-based alternative to the residential childcare institutions where young offenders normally would have been placed away from their families. Until the end of 2000, it was a model financed by the German state lottery. Since the beginning of 2001, it has had a regular contract with the Berlin youth service system, and since that time has worked with families and children of a variety of origins, including Turkish, Lebanese and former Yugoslavian as well as German children, most of them boys. Currently, the project targets young repeat offenders who are under the age of 14 and are suspected of having committed more than six offences against the law during the preceding six months (with a probable minimum sentence of three months for at least one offence if older than 14), or suspected of having committed more than 10 offences during the preceding 12 months (again, with a minimum sentence of three months if older than 14). It is estimated that in Berlin there are between 20 and 40 such children. The offences are mostly theft and robbery, but also include arson, grievous bodily harm, slander and damage of property. More than 60% of these young people refuse to go to school regularly. The children often live in isolated families where parents do not exercise control, where involvement in education is sporadic and where positive role models are few. They are mostly left to themselves and their delinquent peer group becomes more influential as a surrogate for a non-existent family life. Fallschirm is a non-residential project, which works intensively with these young offenders by offering support and alternatives to delinquent behaviours. The project tries to maintain contact, even if the young people are hostile, by seeking to build on the children's strengths and competencies, keeping in regular contact with the family in order to help them to learn to deal with crises and to set boundaries for acceptable behaviours. The project workers work closely with the social services, the school and the parents in order to challenge the ways children can justify their delinquency and encourage them to take responsibility for their actions. The project also tries to get young people back into school and take part in legal leisure-time activities such as youth/sports clubs. The programme includes individual or group leisure activities combined with social skills training and regular sessions with parents to improve their educational skills. Sixty per cent of the children needed to be accompanied to school every morning for several weeks, as well as to the police when necessary. The project is available to the young people 24 hours a day through a hotline. Self-evaluation shows that the project's targets – reducing delinquency and truancy, changing leisure activities and reinforcing parental responsibility – are met in about half of the cases (EUCPN, 2006).

Similar projects were established in the Turin region of Italy in the 1990s. For example, in the town of Giaveno, a voluntary organisation that aimed to encourage vulnerable young adolescents to stay in school set up a neighbourhood centre where young people could come every day. Similar centres were set up by social cooperatives in Moncalieri and the Mirafiori Sud area of Turin. Activities were organised every day for 9- to 15-year-olds who were referred by the local social and health services as a result of educational, family or psychological difficulties. Younger children were targeted by a project called 'Ludoteca', or 'Gameplace'. The project aimed to support nursery schools and families to integrate 3- to 14-year-olds at risk of social exclusion, attracting an average of 70 children every day (Buckland and Stevens, 2001). This approach has something in common with the Danish Family Folk High School, a community-based social and life-skill training programme aimed at 10- to 15-year-olds from minority backgrounds and with the Swedish Peaceful Street project in which unemployed people are trained to become guardians 'with a dual security and mentoring role in deprived areas' (Hazel, 2008, p 41).

Conclusions

While this short overview cannot do justice to the large and constantly developing range of activities undertaken internationally to prevent youth crime, there are perhaps several themes that emerge. First, it is clearly important that projects and programmes do not become a substitute for entitlement to mainstream education, health and social services. Whatever the efficacy of school-based interventions, their positive impact can be undone by structural factors, such as truancy and expulsion rates, cuts in pastoral care and support services, and increasing classroom sizes. Family poverty is always likely to create greater problems for children than are addressable through parental support programmes.

Second, a few countries in Northern Europe have started to implement a programme-based approach, often inspired by US models, sometimes home-grown. While these have a good deal of empirical and theoretical backing, there is a question of how far it will be possible to mainstream such programmes. Other countries seem steadfastly committed to an approach based on social casework and meeting needs as they arise. However, the political and media climate in many countries is increasingly concerned about crime. Consequently, a social casework approach may be hard to sustain, particularly where the intervention thresholds are high and resources for proactive and preventive work are limited.

Third, the danger of labelling and thereby inadvertently reinforcing rather than combating social exclusion is probably greatest with respect to minority ethnic communities. Some of the most interesting projects have attempted to meet the needs of hard-to-reach children, often from ethnic or immigrant minorities. Prisons all over the world show strong overrepresentations of such minorities and developing effective prevention and treatment approaches must be a priority.

Fourth, there is the question of the relationships between the social agencies and the police and criminal justice agencies. Some commentators feel uncomfortable about the presence of police officers in schools, but evidence from the UK suggests that most teachers and pupils like the sense of security it brings. There does seem to be a need for clear rules of engagement when agencies with very different aims and objectives are working together. This is true in relation to some of the police-led attempts to stimulate speedy action in relation to child offenders under the age of criminal responsibility. As far as the minimum age of criminal responsibility is concerned, jurisdictions need to make sure that they respond to the Council of Europe's recommendation that 'culpability should better reflect the age and maturity of the offender, and be more in step with the offender's stage of development, with criminal measures being progressively applied as individual responsibility increases' (Council of Europe, 2003, p 1).

Fifth, important issues arise relating to the practice of prevention work. Some people are uneasy about schemes that mix children who have committed unlawful acts with children who have not (or have not been caught). Mixed groups can try to harness the skills and influence of non-delinquent peers in helping young offenders discover alternative ways of behaving, but run the risk of contamination effects. Clearly, group interventions need to ensure that positive, pro-social norms prevail as far as possible. There are also some concerns that preventive work with children operates mainly on a verbal basis, focusing on conversations with individuals or groups. Detached youth work, arts, music and sport can all be vehicles through which positive relationships can be fostered.

Finally, there are issues relating to the emphasis on cases rather than places, and an argument for more vigorous efforts to increase social capital in the most deprived areas. This requires an approach that concentrates not so much on risks, deficits and so-called 'criminogenic' needs, but focuses instead on identifying and building strengths in individuals, families and communities.

Note
[1] England and Wales only. Rates for the prison population in the UK are: England and Wales: 153 per 100,000; Scotland: 148 per 100,000; Northern Ireland: 86 per 100,000.

References
Allen, R. (2008) 'Crime and social policy', Paper delivered at the ICPA/Norwegian Prison Service Conference on high risk offenders under 18, Oslo, 5 June, www.kcl. ac.uk/depsta/law/research/icps/downloads/Crime%20and%20Social%20Policy. doc

Baldry, A. and Farrington, D. (2007) 'Effectiveness of programs to prevent school bullying', *Victims & Offenders*, vol 2, no 2, pp 183-204.

Buckland, G. and Stevens, A. (2001) *Review of effective practice with young offenders in mainland Europe*, London: YJB.

Council of Europe (2003) *Recommendation (2003)20 of the Committee of Ministers to member states concerning new ways of dealing with juvenile delinquency and the role of juvenile justice*, Strasbourg: Council of Europe.

EUCPN (European Crime Prevention Network) (2006) *A review of good practices in preventing juvenile crime in the European Union*, www.eucpn.org/goodpractice/ showdoc.asp?docid=28

Hazel, N. (2008) *Cross national comparison of youth justice*, London: YJB.

ICPS World Prison Brief, www.prisonstudies.org

Kuuire, R. (2003) 'Finland', in A. Stevens and B. Gladstone (eds) *Learning not offending: Diversion of young people from crime in Europe*, Brasted: RPS Rainer.

Larsson, A. (2005) 'Turning point for children through parents', Presentation to the Cooperation Network around the juvenile offenders, Tallinn, Estonia, www.rikoksentorjunta.fi/uploads/u7fw7yhpp.doc

Ogden, T. and Halliday-Boykins, C.A. (2004) 'Multi-systemic treatment of antisocial adolescents in Norway: replication of clinical outcomes outside of the US', *Child and Adolescent Mental Health*, vol 9, no 2, pp 77-83.

OHCHR (Office of the High Commissioner for Human Rights) (2005) *Report by Alvaro Gil-Robles, Commissioner for Human Rights, on his visit to the United Kingdom, 4-12 November 2004*, Strasbourg: OHCHR.

Olweus, D. (1993) *Bullying at school: What we know and what we can do*, Oxford: Blackwell.

Olweus, D. (1995) *Gewalt in der Schule: Was Lehrer und Eltern wissen sollten – und tun können [Bullying at school: What we know and what we can do]*, Bern: Huber.

Olweus, D. and Limber, S. (1999) *Blueprints for violence prevention: Bullying Prevention Program*, Colorado, BO: Institute of Behavioral Science, University of Colorado.

Petrie, P., Boddy, J., Cameron, C., Heptinstall, E., McQuail, S., Simon, A. and Wigfall, V. (2008) *Pedagogy: A holistic, personal approach to work with children and young people, across services*, London: TCRU Institute of Education.

Schäfer, H. (2004) 'Combating criminal behaviour among children under 14 years of age – the responsibility of the educational system', in Centre for the Prevention of Youth Crime (ed) *Prevention of youth crime in Germany: Educational strategies: Trends, experiences and approaches*, Munich: German Youth Institute.

Stevens, A., Kessler, I. and Gladstone, B. (2006) *Review of good practices in preventing juvenile crime in the European Union*, Canterbury: European Crime Prevention Network.

UN (United Nations) (1990) *Guidelines for the prevention of juvenile delinquency (Riyadh Guidelines)*, Adopted and proclaimed by General Assembly Resolution 45/112 of 14 December 1990, Strasbourg: OHCHR.

UN Committee on the Rights of the Child (2007) *Children's rights in juvenile justice: General comment no 10*, Strasbourg: OHCHR.

UNICEF (United Nations Children's Fund) (2007) *An overview of child well-being in rich countries*, Report Card 7, Florence: Innocenti Research Centre.

Utting, D., Monteiro, H. and Ghate, D. (2007) *Interventions for children at risk of developing antisocial personality disorder*, London: Policy Research Bureau.

von Liszt, F. (1905) 'Das Verbrechen als sozial-pathologische Erscheinung', in F. von Lizst, *Strafrechtliche Aufsätze und Vorträge, Zweiter Band, 1982-1904*, Berlin: J. Guttentag.

Wibord, G. and Hamewinkel, R. (2005) *Eigenstaendig warden: Sucht-und Gewalpraevention in der Schule durch Persoenlichct [Becoming autonomous: prevention of addiction and violence in school by supporting the development of personality]*, Evaluation Sergebnisse der ersten Klassenstufe, www.edu_butler.at/Rotary/docs/EW-Merzer.pdf

Conclusion

Maggie Blyth and Enver Solomon

The contributions in this volume raise important policy questions in relation to early intervention strategies and prevention work with children, young people and their families. In terms of current government policy, it is clear that early intervention has become firmly embedded under New Labour's administration as the overarching strategy to address both social exclusion and offending behaviour among children, young people and their families. While there is no blueprint or absolute definition of early intervention at the national level, there are a number of assumptions underpinning the approach that we set out in the Introduction to this volume. These are that the earlier the intervention, the better it will be, that targeted as opposed to universal provision is appropriate and that coercive engagement based on a carrot-and-stick approach is most effective. Each of these is debated in the wide range of contributions to this volume.

In conclusion, we attempt to chart a path through the contentious intervention field in the context of the reformed youth justice system and its rebalancing during 2008. We consider how the greater integration of youth justice with youth services, children's services and family work allows for a new structure at a local level in which to respond properly to the needs of those young people and families considered most at risk of offending.

During 2008, the government has set out its agenda comprehensively in two key documents. The publication of the *Youth taskforce action plan* in March 2008 (DCSF, 2008) and the Youth crime action plan (YCAP) in July 2008 (HM Government, 2008) reinforces early intervention strategy as fundamental to addressing youth crime and anti-social behaviour (ASB). These documents charge children's services at local level with its implementation. This provides some readjustment for youth justice services, with the investment in prevention moving back firmly into the social care arena although maintaining important criminal justice links. Opportunities for improving educational chances, promoting health intervention and providing safe accommodation for vulnerable children will be important outcomes associated with the Every Child Matters agenda to be firmly embedded in one Children's Plan for each local authority. Increasingly, these outcomes are set within Local Area Agreements to ensure that those children, young people and families most 'at risk' are top priorities for Local Strategic Partnerships.

Joining up youth justice services

Underlying both government action plans published during 2008 there is an assumption that investment in early intervention should coincide with a downturn in the numbers of children entering youth justice and greater public confidence in how crime and ASB is dealt with in local communities. While a coordinated service for children and young people in need is welcomed, it is important that this continues to be multiagency and inclusive of both welfare and criminal justice agencies. It is critical that the shift of emphasis to early intervention as part of children's services should not be at the expense of isolation from criminal justice partners, such as the police, probation and courts, and does not undermine the positive developments of the last decade in relation to information sharing, partnership working and work with victims. A dissolution of these factors is likely to lead to even greater public scepticism about the purpose of the youth justice system and its ability to effectively prevent youth offending.

A potential solution is to be found in linking an early intervention strategy embedded in children's services into an offender management model, aligned to criminal justice agencies. Preventative, targeted work becomes the early stages of a continuum that leads to specialist and intensive work retained for those high-risk young offenders who require the structured surveillance and supervision from specialist practitioners. This framework is one that some Youth Offending Teams (YOTs) are already adopting with partners in youth support services and probation areas through 'integrated offender management'. It allows for early intervention to be undertaken with targeted young people who may not be serving court orders but are involved in ASB, with the merit of linking into 'prevent and deter' measures at the local level.

In configuring new service models, it is of course vital to ensure that lessons are learned from national evaluations of key early intervention work such as family intervention projects (FIPs), parenting programmes, Sure Start and the Youth Inclusion Programme (YIP) in order to prevent more children entering the youth justice system as a result of failed interventions and to prevent those most needy families becoming further marginalised from mainstream services.

Avoiding unintended outcomes

Current government policy considers the early intervention model as essential in addressing harm and vulnerability among young people and this justifies the thrust of prevention work. It also fits neatly with an increasing preoccupation across the public sector with attempting to predict as early as possible the risk factors associated with particular delinquent or ASB. Whatever the positive intentions of early intervention, it is important to be aware of unintended consequences associated with risk management. Young people can be labelled as criminals without ever having committed an offence. One way to prevent these unintended outcomes is to clearly define early intervention at the local level to ensure an appropriate and adequate response to proposed service users. It may well be that in being proactive to the problems facing many marginalised young people and their families, a real and marked impact can be achieved in preventing a drift into offending behaviour. However, this requires a multiagency partnership approach across children's services, health and criminal justice agencies, with incentives for local authorities to invest in early intervention alongside diversionary tactics involving the police. Reducing crime and addressing need are flip-sides of the same coin, albeit couched more formally as safeguarding and public protection measures. If an early intervention approach allows greater integration of safeguarding and public protection then that can only be a step forward for vulnerable young people and their families, either as perpetrators or victims of crime. Howard Williamson (Chapter One) is candid in his conclusion that, so long as local services respond to young people's needs, it does not matter who pays for the support and which profession they originate from.

Indeed, there is persuasive evidence from Felicity de Zulueta's work (Chapter Five) that it is only by responding at an early age that protective factors can be established with children who have been victims of violence or neglect. She places much merit on the Family Nurse Partnership (FNP) and any strategies that identify problems early. However, like Judy Nixon and Sadie Parr, in their analysis of the evaluations of certain family intervention projects (FIPs) (Chapter Three), she stresses the importance of practitioner judgement in working with young people and families, using expertise to enhance relationships and inspire confidence in interventions provided.

Places, not cases

The Every Child Matters reforms have assisted the shift in focus of general children's services towards early intervention and prevention, and in light of the thrust of the YCAP, it seems that youth justice policy and practice will be integrated more fully into children's services, thus leading to more scope for prevention work. Although Youth Justice Board (YJB) initiatives such as Safer Schools Partnerships (police in schools) and the Youth Inclusion Programme (YIP) are examples of early intervention work within the youth justice sphere, as highlighted in this volume, this has led to concerns from some commentators over net-widening and labelling children within a criminal justice arena. Barry Goldson (Chapter Six) makes a strong argument for early diversionary tactics as part of any prevention strategy. He remains adamant in his concluding analysis, that early intervention models serve only to criminalise young people, producing a 'bloated and obese youth justice system' based on 'populist punitiveness'.

The children, young people and families most likely to have contact with the youth justice system are routinely drawn from the most deprived communities and neighbourhoods. As John Pitts points out (Chapter Two), it is neighbourhood provision that must be augmented through early intervention work and carefully commissioned to ensure that it is funded to address broader social, economic and cultural factors. One observation, therefore, is the importance of targeted neighbourhood work, at the local level, rather than merely targeted approaches involving certain identified young people or families. Rob Allen refers to this (Chapter Seven) as the 'emphasis on cases rather than places', a point Karen Clarke draws out (Chapter Four) in her commentary on Sure Start and the new children's centres being extended nationally. It is critical that the development of locality teams link across education, health, housing and with YOTs, police and community safety teams to improve neighbourhoods.

And, as Rob Allen states in his comparison study with international models of preventive work with young people and families (Chapter Seven), it is critical that providing targeted responses does not result in removing young people and their families from mainstream services. He supports an emphasis that tackles intergenerational problems in communities rather than focusing merely on risk.

An effective workforce

All too often for the government the political imperative to show that it is not soft on crime has led to early intervention being captured by an enforcement agenda. This has particularly been the case with some ASB initiatives and has permeated many of the proposals set out in the recent YCAP. Reservations have been expressed in this volume over approaches that seek to coerce people and their families who choose not to engage in services but whose problems continue to be challenging (see Chapters Three, Four and Five, in particular). While the desire to ensure that there will be consequences for those young people and families who do not change their behaviour or make use of intensive support or training such as parenting programmes is understandable, there is a need to balance the danger of the subsequent ASBO or other sanction placing them at greater risk of entering the criminal justice system. The person best placed to make this judgement is the practitioner who is working with the family or young person. They should be given the discretion to decide at what point a tough sanction-led approach would be most beneficial. It is vital that practitioners are given the confidence and training to exercise their professional discretion, with the assistance of statutory assessment tools, within a sensible framework of rewards and sanctions agreed at a local level. Howard Williamson (Chapter One) calls for 'advanced skill youth practitioners' who are sophisticated and experienced in working with the 'complexities of young people's lives'. Politicians who wish to sound tough on crime should be aware of the importance of relationships with key staff in improving the behaviour of challenging children and their families, a message that comes through from the research conducted by Judie Nixon and Sadie Parr into the work of FIPs (see Chapter Three). Enforcement of court orders is clearly necessary but discretion should be used to determine the nature and scale of enforcement outside the criminal justice arena.

Where next?

The shared responsibility for youth justice by the Ministry of Justice and the Department for Children, Schools and Families (DCSF) has not brought the clarity of governance and balanced approach many predicted in 2007, and this has led to continuing polarised views on how youth justice services should address both public protection matters and prevention. The YCAP moves responsibility for youth justice towards the DCSF, and with YOTs beginning to integrate with targeted youth support services within children's trust arrangements, there may now be the opportunity to develop early intervention approaches that invest in a range of preventive services for young people and their families. This should serve not just to reduce the risks young people present to themselves, to victims of crime and to the wider community but should also meet their needs more effectively.

What are the key lessons for policy makers and practitioners in relation to early intervention?

First, although it is not new for youth justice services to straddle the gulf between welfare and risk, now is the time for a more sophisticated approach to ensure that children and young people who offend remain the key priorities of children's services. Governance arrangements between children's trusts and YOTs must be clear and maintained with Crime and Disorder Reduction Partnerships. Increasing joint commissioning should occur between children's services and criminal justice agencies to test the evidence base of early intervention. The YCAP paves the way for these agreements.

Second, an experienced and trained workforce is essential to foster effective relationships with young people at risk to ensure that non-engagement does not lead to more marginalisation and offending behaviour. The skills required to build positive relationships with young people and local communities should not be underestimated. There are lessons to be learned from the national evaluations of FIPs and parenting work. There are workforce development opportunities in merging YOT business with youth work.

Third there needs to be greater recognition of the importance of places as opposed to simply focusing on cases. Effective prevention strategies require work not only with individuals and their families but also with the communities in which they live. This requires greater investment in neighbourhood renewal and mechanisms to enable active community involvement in prevention programmes.

Finally, without rigorous evaluation of early intervention projects, key learning will not be distributed to those designing services and working directly with young people and their families. As the contributions in this volume suggest, there is a clear evidence base for early intervention but there are also contentious issues to be considered if the government is serious about reducing the numbers of children and young people entering the youth justice system or going on to reoffend.

References

DCSF (Department for Children, Schools and Families) (2008) *Youth taskforce action plan: Give respect, get respect*, London: DCSF.

HM Government (2008) *Youth crime action plan 2008*, London: COI.